D0761228

# Poverty and Social Assistance in Transition Countries

# Poverty and Social Assistance in Transition Countries

Jeanine Braithwaite
Christiaan Grootaert
Branko Milanovic

St. Martin's Press
New York

ISBN 0-312-22436-2

Library of Congress Cataloging-in-Publication Data

Braithwaite, Jeanine.
   Poverty and social assistance in transition countries / Jeanine
Braithwaite, Christiaan Grootaert, Branko Milanovic
      p. cm.
   Includes bibliographical references and index.
   ISBN 0-312-22436-2 (cloth)
   1. Poverty—Europe, Eastern.   2. Poverty—Former Soviet republics.
3. Europe, Eastern—Economic conditions—1989–   4. Former Soviet
republics—Economic conditions.   5. Europe, Eastern—Social policy.
6. Former Soviet republics—Social policy.   I. Grootaert,
Christiaan, 1950– .   II. Milanovic, Branko.   III. Title.
HC244.Z9P613   2000
362.5'8'091724—dc21
                                                                99–37662
                                                                    CIP

Design by Binghamton Valley Composition

First edition: March, 2000
10 9 8 7 6 5 4 3 2 1

# CONTENTS

# ACKNOWLEDGMENTS

WE WOULD LIKE TO THANK Robert Ackland, Mark Foley, Thesia Garner, Gi-Taik Oh, Sandor Sipos, Sasoun Tsirounian, and Yvonne Ying for their assistance in preparing and using the database, and Susan Assaf, Precy Lizarondo and Gracie Ochieng for their assistance with document processing. Financial support from the World Bankís Research Committee is gratefully acknowledged. The findings, interpretation, and conclusions expressed in this study are entirely those of the authors and should not be attributed in any manner to the World Bank, to its affiliated organizations, or to members of its Board of Executive Directors or the countries they represent.

# PREFACE

THIS BOOK IS THE PRODUCT OF RESEARCH on determinants of poverty and targeting of social assistance in Eastern Europe and the former Soviet Union (FSU). The research was done during the years 1996 and 1997, using household budget surveys from six transition countries for the period 1993–95.

The motivation for this research lies in the increased interest exhibited in the transition economies as well as in the World Bank in issues of (what is in the economic jargon called) "targeting," that is, in improving the delivery of social assistance so that it reaches those who need it. This increased interest stems from the current emphasis on poverty reduction and social equity within the World Bank and its member governments, as well as from financial constraints faced by most transition countries' governments that make the continuation of the provision of a quasi-universal social safety net unaffordable.

Our key objective was to try to make meaningful policy recommendations on how to improve targeting. But in order to do so, we must know whom to target, that is, who are the poor. Thus, after a brief discussion of the countries included in the study in Chapter 1, we analyze in Chapter 2 the determinants of poverty in the selected transition economies. We study whether poverty is associated with specific demographic traits and economic characteristics and whether these characteristics are more or less similar across the transition economies. Our objective in Chapter 2 is to derive relatively robust conclusions regarding the factors that are linked with poverty, how important they are, and if and why they differ among the countries. These conclusions have direct policy implications for (1) targeting by indicators (e.g., by family size or region); (2) the role of education in reducing poverty; (3) the importance of unemployment as an explanator of poverty (as opposed to, for example, the working poor).

In Chapter 3, we discuss the targeting of social assistance. In all countries, social assistance offices have a certain income cutoff point, whether official or de facto, which they use to screen those who are eligible for social assistance from those who are not. Taking this cutoff point, our objective is to investigate if there are systematic biases against or in favor of certain household types. For example, if for a given income level rural households have systematically a lower chance to be helped, then there is a pro-urban bias in the system. The cause of this bias, for example, unequal allocation of government money between rural and urban areas, greater importance of unrecorded incomes in villages, lack of rural population's knowledge about the available social assistance, or some other factor, can be investigated through field visits. Policy conclusions regarding the possible improvements in the delivery of social assistance thus combine the results derived from the desk study based on the survey data, and field work.

In order to study these topics, a very large and standardized data base has been constructed using household- and individual-level data from the existing income and expenditure surveys. The surveys were conducted over the period 1993–95. The countries included in the study were originally eight. Four are East European countries: Hungary (date of survey: 1993), Bulgaria (1995), Poland (1993), and Slovakia (1993). Four were part of the former Soviet Union: Estonia (1995) in the Baltics, Armenia (1994) in the Caucasus, the Kyrgyz republic (1993) in Central Asia, and Russia (1993–94). For all the countries except Armenia, the Kyrgyz republic, and Russia, we used the official survey data collected by the countries' statistical offices. For the Kyrgyz republic and Russia, we used the living standards surveys partly financed by the World Bank. For Armenia, we used a household survey produced by the State Committee on Statistics and the Yerevan University Department of Sociology.

In selecting the countries to study, our first requirement was to have access to the individual- and household-level data from a nationally representative survey. The task was then to make the variables as comparable as possible across the countries, by ensuring either that a given variable (e.g., wage income, food expenditure, education level, housing ownership) is defined the same way in each country survey, or if this was not possible, to document clearly the definitional differences. During the exacting and lengthy process of variable standardization, we found ourselves compelled to drop two countries—Armenia and Slovakia—from the analysis because of what we consider to be potentially serious flaws within the surveys themselves, or inconsistencies between the variable definitions in the two surveys and other surveys that could not be overcome.[1]

The entire database, referred by the acronym HEIDE (Household Expenditure and Income Data for Transition Economies) is in STATA format. It contains 72 "standardized" variables[2] for the eight countries, and is available from the World Bank (for a small fee, needed to cover reproduction costs).[3]

# CHAPTER 1

# THE TRANSITION ECONOMIES IN THE STUDY: *How Similar and Different They Are*

BRANKO MILANOVIC

## 1.1 A BRIEF SURVEY OF THE COUNTRIES INCLUDED IN THE STUDY

The six countries included in our study are very diverse, even if they all belong to "transition" economies, that is, are moving from a state-dominated to a private market economy. Three are East European countries: Hungary, Bulgaria, and Poland. Three were part of the former Soviet Union but have, however, very different income levels, cultural heritage, and proportion of urban population. They are Estonia in the Baltics, the Kyrgyz republic in Central Asia, and Russia.

To give the reader an idea of the diversity of the countries we shall contrast them across several dimensions: first, by using generally available macroeconomic data (Section 1.2), and then by using the data derived from household budget surveys (Section 1.3). Among the macroeconomic variables, we chose population size and density; gross domestic product (GDP) level; type of transition policies implemented; inflation rate during the surveys; and spending on social transfers. Why did we choose these variables? Population shows the relative importance of the country for the poverty reduction in the region (a given percentage decrease in the head count poverty index brings out of poverty more people in a more populous country). The level of GDP summarizes the difference in the level of development. The rates of inflation shows us what are the potential pitfalls faced by the statistical agencies when gathering (nominal) income and expenditure information, and by researchers when they use the data. The type of transition (relatively slow or fast), and the initial conditions before the transition allow us to see if the countries included cover the entire range of transition experiences. The share of social transfers in GDP gives us a first approximation as to how redistributive the system is, that is, whether we can expect the poor to be more numerous or less for a given relative poverty line (a topic discussed in Chapter 2).

## Population

The HEIDE countries (called HEIDE from the name of the data set Household Expenditure and Income Data for Transition Economies) span in terms of population the whole range among post-Communist countries, going from Russia, with almost 150 million people, to Estonia, the smallest country to emerge from the Soviet Union, with one-hundredth of Russia's population. In between is Poland, with a population of almost 40 million, Hungary and Bulgaria, with 8 million–10 million, and the Kyrgyz republic, with a population of 4.5 million (Table 1.1).

Two East European countries (Poland and Hungary) have relatively high population densities, exceeding 100 people per square kilometer or about the same as France, but half the density of the United Kingdom and Germany, and only a fourth that of the Netherlands (425).[1] Bulgaria's population density is less than 100, while Estonia and the Kyrgyz republic have much lower densities (33 and 23), not very different from that of the United States (28). Russia, of course, has the lowest population density among the countries in the sample (9).

**Table 1.1.** **Population indicators**

| Country | Population size 1995 (millions) | Population density (persons per km²) | Population growth rate (% p.a. 1985–95) |
|---|---|---|---|
| Russia | 148.2 | 9 | 0.3 |
| Poland | 38.6 | 123 | 0.4 |
| Hungary | 10.3 | 110 | –0.3 |
| Bulgaria | 8.4 | 77 | –0.6 |
| Kyrgyz republic | 4.5 | 23 | 1.2 |
| Estonia | 1.5 | 33 | –0.3 |

*Source*: *World Bank Atlas 1997*. Countries ranked by population size.

All countries except the Kyrgyz republic have very low positive (under half a percent per year) or even negative long-term population growth rates. The most recent period has been even worse in terms of population growth, as, for example, in the case of Russia, which has experienced a population decrease of about 0.5 percent per year since 1991.

## Income Levels

Table 1.2 shows per capita GDPs in the year when the household budget surveys were conducted, and in 1993 when the most recent round of *International comparison project* was done. The first values are in current dollars, the second in dollars of equal purchasing power parity ($PPP), that is, in international dollars. Measured in $PPP, the HEIDE countries' GDPs per capita range from little more than $2,000 (Kyrgyz republic) to $7,100 (for Hungary). Even the richest HEIDE country's income is only about a third of the European Union (EU) average ($PPP 20,400). The poorest EU country (Greece) is almost twice as rich as the richest HEIDE country.[2] In current dollar terms, the HEIDE countries' GDPs are of course less (because the price level in these countries is lower than the world price level and/or their currencies are undervalued). The per capita GDPs in current dollars range from the improbably low of $200 per year in the Kyrgyz republic to about $3,700 in Hungary. The very low value for the Kyrgyz republic was a result of the severely under-

**Table 1.2.    GDP per capita and infant mortality**

| Country (year of survey) | GDP per capita in 1993 (in $PPP) | GDP per capita in current $ (year of survey) | Infant mortality (per 10,000) |
|---|---|---|---|
| Hungary (93) | 7,100 | 3,700 | 11 |
| Russia (93–94) | 5,900 | 2,000 | 18 |
| Poland (93) | 5,600 | 2,200 | 14 |
| Bulgaria (95) | 5,000 | 1,500 | 15 |
| Estonia (95) | 4,500 | 2,400 | 14 |
| Kyrgyz rep. (93) | 2,400a/ | 200 | 30 |

*Note*: All GDP per capita rounded off to the nearest hundred. Countries ranked by their GDP per capita (in $PPP).
a/ From *World Bank Atlas 1995*.
*Source*: GDP per capita in $PPP: *International comparison project* 1993. GDP per capita in current dollars: World Bank database. Infant mortality from *World Development Report 1997*.

valued currency in the survey year. In effect, in 1995, which is only two years after the survey, the Kyrgyz per capita GDP in the current dollars was almost double while real per capita GDP had increased by only 4 percent. This is why the use of $PPP values gives us a much more accurate estimate of the countries' actual standard of living than the use of current dollar values (and particularly so for the transition economies, given that all have experienced wide swings in their real exchange rates).

Another strong indicator of the country's level of development is the infant mortality rate (see Table 1.2). The rates range from low 11 in Hungary,[3] to a fairly high 18 for Russia, and to an extremely high 30 for the Kyrgyz republic—and even these high rates might be underestimates (see Kingkade, 1993).

## Type of Transition

All countries but Hungary undertook a radical stabilization that normally included slashing consumer subsidies and the fiscal deficit, liberalizing prices and the exchange rate, and opening up trade. The stabilization programs were undertaken between January 1990 (the

**Table 1.3. Transition speed and outcomes**

| Country (year of survey) | Cumulative liberalization index (1994) | Date of "big bang" stabilization program | Decline in real GDP between 1987 and year of survey (in % of the 1987 GDP) |
|---|---|---|---|
| Poland (93) | 4.14 | January 1990 | 9 |
| Hungary (93) | 4.11 | None | 17 |
| Estonia (95) | 2.93 | End 1991 | 33 |
| Bulgaria (95) | 2.90 | February 1991 | 22 |
| Russia (93–94) | 1.92 | January 1992 | 31 |
| Kyrgyz rep. (93) | 1.81 | January 1992 | 22 |

*Note*: Countries ranked by their CLI.
*Source*: CLI from de Melo, Denizer, and Gelb (1996); World Bank (DECRG) database.

Polish program, the earliest one in the entire region) and early 1992 (see Table 1.3). Thus, by the time our surveys were conducted (1993–1995) all countries had between two and four years of post-stabilization experience. The surveys therefore did capture the full (early) effects of the transition.

The existence of the stabilization program alone is an imperfect measure of the actual depth of reforms. This is because it is not only the strength of current reforms that matters but also the strength and duration of past reforms. We measure this aspect by using the cumulative liberalization index (CLI) calculated by de Melo, Denizer, and Gelb (1996). The index measures the cumulative sum of the reforms over the period 1989–1994 in three areas: privatization, liberalization of the internal market (prices, trading), and liberalization of foreign trade and investments. As the authors of the index point out, the index can be regarded as a measure of behavioral changes stimulated by the overall (past and present) policy reforms. Its values are reported in Table 1.3. Poland, thanks to its history of reforms and a strong stabilization program in 1990, and Hungary, owing principally to its sustained—even if non-dramatic—reforms, have the highest CLI values. Poland and Hungary belong to the group of "advanced" reformers (as defined by de Melo, Denizer, and Gelb [1996]); Estonia and Bulgaria are "high-intermediate" reformers, and Russia and the Kyrgyz republic are "low-intermediate" reformers. No HEIDE country is in the "slow" reformers group.

Three out of six countries are "new" countries in the sense that they came into existence after the breakup of the Soviet Union. These countries faced greater problems than others, because in addition to the usual problems of transition from a planned to market economy, they had to deal with problems caused by the disruption of trade. Table 1.3 shows the declines in real GDP experienced by the HEIDE countries between 1987 and the year of survey. Indeed the countries of the former Soviet Union all declined more than those of Eastern Europe. The "advanced reformers" (Poland and Hungary) had, by 1993 (the survey year), GDP levels that were, respectively, 9 and 17 percent less than in 1987. "Intermediate reformers," be they "high" or "low," declined by between 22 and 31 percent.

## Inflation

Low inflation is very important for the precision of reporting in the surveys. Despite the fact that all income and expenditure amounts in four surveys (Polish, Estonian, Kyrgyz, and Russian) are reported in constant prices, the presence of high rates of inflation makes such adjustment often very difficult and subject to error. The survey results consequently become less reliable. This is because the price indexes one normally uses as deflators are monthly, and a given nominal income, or expenditure incurred at the beginning or at the end of the month is treated as same in real terms. However with a rate of inflation of 30 to 50 or more percent per month these amounts are indeed very different in real terms. Among our countries, the problem might have been serious in Russia and the Kyrgyz republic, where inflation rates over the survey period were, respectively, 15 and 27 percent per month (see Table 1.4).

Household surveys in Bulgaria and Hungary do not make any adjustment for inflation: they simply use nominal values even if the Hungarian survey covers an entire year. Fortunately, Hungary also had a relatively low *yearly* rate of inflation (23 percent per annum) while inflation in Bulgaria in the first half of 1995 (the survey period) was 15 percent.

**Table 1.4. Inflation during the survey period**

| Country | Average monthly inflation over the survey period (%) | Inflation over the period of the survey (%) | Period of the HBS survey |
|---|---|---|---|
| Estonia | 1.6 | 5 | Q3:1995 |
| Hungary | 1.7 | 23 | 1993 |
| Bulgaria | 2.4 | 15 | H1:1995 |
| Poland | 2.5 | 16 | H1:1993 |
| Russia | 15.4 | 105 | Oct. 93–Feb 94 |
| Kyrgyz republic | 27.3 | 62 | Oct–Nov. 1993 |

*Note*: Q3:1995 denotes third quarter of 1995; H1:1995 denotes the first half of 1995. Countries ranked by monthly inflation over the survey period.
*Source*: World Bank (DECRG) database.

## Social Transfers

The relative importance of social cash transfers among HEIDE countries varies from more than 20 percent of GDP (Hungary) to 9 percent (Russia). All East European countries spend more in terms of GDP than the countries of the former Soviet Union (Table 1.5). The largest chunk is, of course, accounted for by pensions: between 6 and 15 percent of GDP. Spending on family benefits and social assistance ranges between 2 percent (in Bulgaria) and 5 percent (in Hungary). The varying importance of social transfers in the countries' GDP may (to some extent) affect comparability among the HEIDE countries. This is not only because the countries with larger transfers may be expected to have fewer poor when we use a country-adjusted poverty line (as in Chapter 2). Another effect appears when we study in Chapter 3 the types of social assistance regimes in each country and their targeting characteristics. Countries with large indicator-based, non-income-tested social programs like pensions, unemployment benefits, and family benefits may exhibit different features in their social assistance programs from the countries that have relatively small entitlement programs. For countries with large entitlement programs, social assistance can be relatively small (being as it were crowded out by other social programs) and its targeting, whether good or bad, may be of little relevance for most of the pop-

**Table 1.5.    Social cash transfers**
**(as percent of GDP; in the year of survey)**

| Country (year of survey) | Pensions | Family benefits and social assistance | All other cash social transfers | Total cash transfers |
|---|---|---|---|---|
| Hungary (93) | 11.2 | 4.7 | 4.2 | 20.1 |
| Poland (93) | 14.9 | 2.3 | 1.7 | 18.9 |
| Bulgaria (95) | 8.3 | 1.8 | 1.7 | 11.8 |
| Estonia (95) | 7.2 | 2.6 | 0.3 | 10.1 |
| Kyrgyz republic (93) | 6.7 | 2.8 | n.a. | 9.5 |
| Russia (93–94) | 5.8 | 2.5 | 0.9 | 9.2 |

*Note*: Countries ranked by the share of total cash social transfers in GDP.
*Source*: World Bank (DECRG) data.

ulation. For other countries, however, it is on the social assistance that the brunt of the anti-poverty role is placed. It is important to see how social assistance programs function because efficiency or lack of it may have significant impact on poverty statistics and social, and even political, support of the reforms.

# 1.2. DIFFERENCES AMONG THE COUNTRIES (AS REVEALED BY HOUSEHOLD BUDGET SURVEYS)

In this section, we contrast the countries included in our study across several dimensions using the data obtained from household budget surveys. We consider four such dimensions: the labor market status of individuals, including the rate of unemployment at the time of survey; the education attainment of the population; the average level of expenditures per equivalent adult (in comparable PPP dollars); and inequality in distribution of welfare (expenditures). The first three variables have their counterparts among the generally available macro data, and we shall compare the results from our surveys with the data gathered from other sources. The data on distribution, however, require access to household information: these data cannot be obtained from any macroeconomic statistics.

**Table 1.6.  Labor market status of household heads and individuals over 14 years (percent)**

|  | Estonia | Hungary | Kyrgyz republic | Poland | Russia |
|---|---|---|---|---|---|
| *Household heads* | | | | | |
| Employed | 61.9 | 59.3 | 70.0 | 62.5 | 64.9 |
| Unemployed | 6.1 | 5.0 | 7.8 | 2.2 | 4.0 |
| Inactive | 32.0 | 35.7 | 22.2 | 35.3 | 31.1 |
| Total | 100.0 | 100.0 | 100.0 | 100.0 | 100.0 |
| | | | | | |
| *Individuals (>14 yrs)* | | | | | |
| Employed | 54.0 | 41.6 | 52.8 | 45.3 | 55.7 |
| Unemployed | 6.0 | 9.6 | 9.3 | 6.8 | 4.1 |
| Inactive | 40.0 | 48.8 | 37.9 | 47.9 | 40.2 |
| Total | 100.0 | 100.0 | 100.0 | 100.0 | 100.0 |
| | | | | | |
| Rate of unemployment (%; from HEIDE household surveys) | 10.0 | 18.8 | 15.0 | 13.1 | 6.9 |
| Official rate of unemployment at the time of survey (%) a/ | 8.7 | 12.9 | n.a. | 14.2 | 5.5 |

*Note*: HBS-based rate of unemployment is defined as the ratio of unemployed individuals over the sum of employed and unemployed. No data on labor force status are available for Bulgaria.

a/ Based on registered unemployed except in Russia and Estonia where the rate is based on labor force surveys.

*Source*: World Bank (DECRG) database except for Estonia: labor force survey data reported in Estonian *Statistical Yearbook 1997*, p. 188.

## Labor Market Status

Unemployment among household heads varied from 2.2 percent in Poland to 6.1 percent in Estonia (see Table 1.6). However, these statistics are misleading because the definition of the household head varied among the countries. In Estonia, the Kyrgyz republic, and Russia the household head was defined as a male in the active age, that is, between 14 and 65 years (if one existed in the household). Thus the results for these three countries give in reality information about the unemployment rate among working-age men. In Hungary and Poland, on the other hand, the household head was defined as the main earner. Since an unemployed member is unlikely to be the main earner, this explains very low rates of unemployment among household heads in these two countries.

Information on the labor force status of all individuals older than 14 years is more reliable. The rates of unemployment range from almost 19 percent in Hungary to 7 percent in Russia. These rates are, except for Hungary, within 1–2 percentage points of the "official" rates for the same period based either on the registered unemployment or special labor force surveys.

## Education

Educational attainment seems to be higher in the republics of the former Soviet Union and Bulgaria than in Central European countries. Thus, for example, although Hungary has a per capita GDP (see Table 1.3) that is some 50 percent above Estonia's and an expenditure per equivalent adult some 20 percent above Estonia's (Table 1.8 below), it has significantly worse education statistics: fewer than 8 percent of individuals have university education in Hungary compared to 12.4 for Estonia (Table 1.7). The Kyrgyz republic, rather unexpectedly, and Russia have the best statistics, with almost 20 and 15 percent of individuals, respectively, with a university education.

However, if educational attainment is assessed in terms of estimated average number of years of education the situation changes somewhat. Poland and Bulgaria now swap places. Poland's high average number of years of education is due to a very high share of people with vocational education (34 percent), very similar to that of Russia and much higher than in other countries. In consequence, Poland's estimated average number of years of education is almost 10 while Bulgaria and Hungary have 9 and 9.4 years. For comparison, the average number of years of education in the United States is 12.3, while in Western European countries it ranges between 10.5 and 12.

**Table 1.7. Education attainment of individuals over 14 years of age (percent)**

|  | Hungary | Bulgaria | Estonia | Poland | Kyrgyz republic | Russia |
|---|---|---|---|---|---|---|
| *Individuals (>14 yrs)* |  |  |  |  |  |  |
| Primary or less | 47.8 | 43.9 | 32.0 | 33.9 | 35.5 | 29.4 |
| Secondary | 22.7 | 35.6 | 55.6ᵃ/ | 24.8 | 26.6 | 21.8 |
| Vocational/technical | 20.8 | 7.5 |  | 34.0 | 18.2 | 34.2 |
| University | 8.7 | 12.9 | 12.4 | 7.4 | 19.8 | 14.7 |
| Total | 100.0 | 100.0 | 100.0 | 100.0 | 100.0 | 100.0 |
| Estimated average number of years of education | 9.0 | 9.4 | 9.8 | 9.9 | 10.3 | 10.5 |

*Note*: The estimated average number of years of education based on the following calculation: for primary school or less, 5 years (to account for those who have fewer than 8 years of primary); for secondary and vocational/technical, 12 years; for university, 16 years. Countries are arranged from left to right according to the estimated average number of years of education.

a/ Includes both secondary and vocational/technical education.

## Expenditure Levels

By measuring household expenditures in purchasing power parity (PPP) terms, we can, as we have done for GDP per capita levels, make cross-country comparisons of the levels of welfare (Table 1.8). Hungary has the highest overall expenditures per equivalent adult ($PPP 412 per month), followed by Bulgaria and Poland ($PPP 310–360) and Russia and Estonia (at $PPP 270–280). The Kyrgyz republic is the poorest with less than $PPP 100. This ranking remains unchanged if we use expenditure per capita. It thus differs somewhat from the ranking of countries according to the GDP per capita (see Table 1.9), mostly because expenditures per capita in Bulgaria and Estonia are (relatively) higher than their GDP per capita levels.

The last line in Table 1.8 gives the ratio between the survey expenditures and disposable income. Only in Poland are expenditures less than income (as might be expected in "normal" circum-

**Table 1.8.**  **Household expenditures per equivalent adult, by component, and household income per equivalent adult (in $PPP; per month)**

|  | Bulgaria | Estonia | Hungary | Poland | Kyrgyz Republic | Russia |
|---|---|---|---|---|---|---|
| Food | 180 | 135 | 137 | 125 | 60 | 155 |
| Housing | 94 | 49 | 129 | 54 | 6 | 6 |
| Education/culture | 14 | 11 | 21 | 18 | 0.2 | 3 |
| Health | 4 | 6 | 15 | 20 | 2 | 2 |
| Transport/communication | 13 | 15 | 42 | 26 | 6 | 5 |
| Clothing | 13 | 25 | 28 | 21 | 6 | 42 |
| Private transfers | 8 | 5 | 8 | n.a. | 2 | 8 |
| Other | 35 | 19 | 33 | 31 | 4 | 31 |
| Home consumption | a/ | 19 | a/ | 13 | 8 | 19 |
| *Total expenditures* | *362* | *285* | *412* | *308* | *94* | *271* |
| Memo: Expenditure per capita | 255 | 194 | 297 | 213 | 56 | 194 |
| Income per capita | 206 | 190 | 278 | 229 | 24 | 130 |
| Expenditure/Income | 1.24 | 1.02 | 1.07 | 0.93 | 2.33 | 1.50 |

*Note*: One $PPP in survey period is 19.9 leva in Bulgaria, 5 EEK in Estonia, 40 forint in Hungary, 6675.4 zloty in Poland, 298.6 ruble in Russia. These values are obtained by indexing the 1993 *International Comparison Project* estimates of the purchasing power exchange rate reported in European Comparison Project (1996) by consumer price inflation between 1993 (average annual level) and the time of survey; except for the Kyrgyz republic where the ratio between the 1993 GDP at current and international dollars (0.34; see World Bank Atlas 1995) is used as a proxy for the ratio between domestic and world prices giving the $PPP exchange rate of 2.38 som. Disposable income is income after government cash transfers and direct taxes.
a/ Home consumption included in food expenditures.

stances); in Hungary and Estonia, expenditures are, respectively, 2 and 7 percent higher than disposable income, while in Bulgaria and Russia, expenditures are one-fourth and one-half greater than disposable income. In the Kyrgyz republic, expenditures are more than double disposable income.

How well do HEIDE expenditures correspond with the expenditures reported in countries' national accounts for the survey year? As shown in Table 1.9, expenditures reported in household budget surveys account, on average, for three-quarters of national account

**Table 1.9.  Comparison expenditures per capita from national accounts and HEIDE data sets**

| Country (survey year) | Expenditure per capita (national account data; $ p.a.) | Expenditures per capita (HEIDE data; $ p.a.) | Ratio: HEIDE to national accounts (in percent) |
|---|---|---|---|
| Hungary (1993) | 2178 | 1551 | 71 |
| Russia (1993) | 385 | 307 | 80 |
| Poland (1993) | 1476 | 986 | 67 |
| Bulgaria (1995) | 1091 | 921 | 84 |
| Estonia (1995) | 1443 | 1050 | 73 |
| Kyrgyz rep. (1993) | 128 | 135 | 105 |
| Unweighted average | 1117 | 825 | 74 |

*Note*: HEIDE expenditures for Russia and the Kyrgyz republic, which are reported in, respectively, October and November 1993 prices, are re-expressed in average yearly prices. *Source*: Hungary: *Statistical Yearbook 1996*, p. 248. Russia: *Rossiya v tsifrach* 1997, p. 138. Poland: *Statistical Yearbook 1996*. Bulgaria: *Statistical Yearbook 1996*, p. 380. Estonia: IMF, *International Financial Statistics: 1997 Yearbook*. Kyrgyz republic: World Bank, *National Accounts of Former Soviet Union Republics* 1996.

expenditures, with the proportion ranging from 67 percent (in Poland) to slightly more than 100 percent (in the Kyrgyz republic).

In terms of expenditure components, food expenditures are about the same in all countries (except the Kyrgyz republic), averaging $PPP 150 per adult equivalent per month (Table 1.8). Thus they account for 33 percent of all expenditures in relatively rich Hungary and 57 percent in relatively poor Russia.[4] Russia has exceptionally low (imputed) expenditures on housing (probably reflecting the continuing high subsidization of utilities and rents)[5] and education and culture. It has, on the other hand, very high expenditures on clothing. In effect, Russia's expenditure pattern is quite different from other countries' (except, to some extent, the Kyrgyz republic's). For all countries except Russia and the Kyrgyz republic, the *average* difference in the percentage shares of the nine expenditures categories listed in Table 1.8 is less than 2 percent.[6] On the other hand, the expenditure shares of Russia and the Kyrgyz republic differ from all East European countries by more than 3 percent; they differ by more than 2 percent from Estonia's pattern, and even the difference between

Russia and the Kyrgyz republic is a relatively high 1.7 percent (i.e., twice as great, for example, as the distance between Poland and Hungary).

Spending on health is the highest in Hungary and Poland, due to more advanced fee recovery and privatized health care. Private transfers given vary in all countries within a very narrow range of $PPP 5–8 per month.[7] Home consumption in Russia, Estonia, and the Kyrgyz republic is about 10 percent of total expenditures; its share is less than 5 percent in Poland.

Not surprisingly, expenditure per equivalent adult in all countries are the highest in the capital (see Figure 1.1). The greatest difference between the capital city and the country as a whole is reported in Russia and the Kyrgyz republic where Moscow and St. Petersburg, and Bishkek have an expenditure level respectively 46 and 58 percent higher than the national average. Expenditures are also everywhere higher in urban than in rural areas. Rural areas' expenditures are some 10 to 15 percent below national averages with the exception of Hungary, which appears to be, in terms of regional welfare differences, the most homogeneous country in the sample. In Poland, Russia, and Bulgaria, survey prices are regionally adjusted so that one source of possible bias against rural areas (that is, that lower recorded expenditures are not so in real terms because the price level is lower) cannot apply.

## Distribution of Expenditures

Inequality in the distribution of equalized expenditures (welfare) is the lowest in Poland and Hungary with the Ginis of under 25 (Table 1.10). These two countries are followed by Bulgaria and Estonia (Ginis between 28 and 30). Russia and the Kyrgyz republic have exceptionally high inequalities, with the Gini coefficients around 40 for Russia and above 40 for the Kyrgyz republic—levels that are more commonly associated with Latin American than former socialist countries. If inequality is measured by inequality of disposable income, the ranking of the countries is the same. In all countries, except Hungary, inequality in income is greater than inequality in expenditures (as is normally the case). Hungary indeed

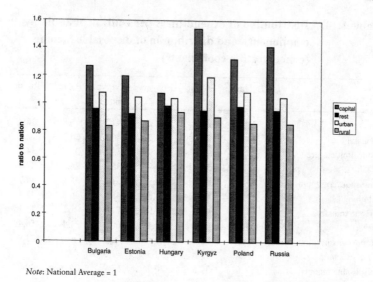

Note: National Average = 1

**Figure 1.1: Relative expenditures per equivalent adult by location**

displays very low levels of both income and expenditure inequality (Ginis of 20 and 21).

Turning to the distribution of individual expenditure components, it is noticeable that the Kyrgyz republic shows an extreme, and possibly unrealistically high, inequality for all components except home consumption. Food, being a necessity, has an elasticity of less than 1 with respect to total expenditures or income in all countries (and the concentration coefficient of food is less than the Gini for total expenditures or disposable income). However, it is noticeable that in Russia and the Kyrgyz republic, and somewhat less in Estonia and Bulgaria, the elasticity of food consumption is not much below unity. This would seem to indicate that, across most of the distribution, a given percentage increase in overall expenditures or income is accompanied by an almost same percentage increase in food expenditures. This is a characteristic of very poor populations.

Education and culture is a luxury (elasticity in excess of 1) in all countries except in Russia and the Kyrgyz republic. So is clothing, and transport and communication in all countries. Expenditures on

Table 1.10.   Distribution of expenditures per equivalent adult, by
              components, and distribution of disposable income
              (concentration coefficients)

| | Bulgaria | Estonia | Hungary | Kyrgyz republic | Poland | Russia |
|---|---|---|---|---|---|---|
| Food | 21.9 | 24.3 | 14.2 | 41.5 | 16.9 | 36.7 |
| Housing | 33.4 | 25.2 | 20.2 | 44.1 | 26.7 | 12.5 |
| Education/culture | 34.4 | 41.1 | 33.9 | 32.3 | 37.7 | 34.5 |
| Health | 18.3 | 33.9 | 23.2 | 35.6 | 28.8 | 27.7 |
| Transport/communication | 43.9 | 48.6 | 48.9 | 51.6 | 38.6 | 44.7 |
| Clothing | 33.4 | 44.7 | 31.6 | 45.9 | 36.8 | 47.4 |
| Private transfers | 48.2 | 44.6 | 25.9 | 71.5 | n.a. | 45.1 |
| Other | 29.8 | 45.8 | 20.4 | 60.2 | 31.1 | 56.4 |
| Home consumption | n.a. | 18.5 | n.a. | 23.7 | n.a. | 23.9 |
| *Total expenditures* | *27.9* | *29.8* | *21.3* | *42.5* | *24.3* | *39.6* |
| Disposable income | 30.3 | 34.5 | 20.2 | 53.7 | 25.9 | 40.0 |
| Difference in inequality between expenditures and disposable income[a] | –2.4 | –4.7 | +0.9 | –11.2 | –1.6 | –0.4 |

*Note*: All values are concentration coefficients (when individuals are ranked by their house-hold's per equivalent adult expenditures), except for the Gini coefficients for total expendi-tures and disposable income. All values are multiplied by 100.
a/ In Gini points.

transport and communication are actually the most elastic of all components. Private transfers are also a luxury everywhere: rich people are more likely to spend a greater share of their expenditures on helping others than the poor are. Home consumption is, on the other hand, even more so than food, very important among the poor.

# CHAPTER 2

# THE DETERMINANTS OF POVERTY IN EASTERN EUROPE AND THE FORMER SOVIET UNION

CHRISTIAAN GROOTAERT AND
JEANINE BRAITHWAITE

## 2.1. INTRODUCTION

This chapter undertakes a comparative analysis of poverty in three East European countries (Bulgaria, Hungary, Poland) and three countries of the former Soviet Union (FSU) (Estonia, Kyrgyz republic, Russia), using the HEIDE database discussed in the preface.

Although our analysis of the HEIDE data found elements in common, the most striking result is how different the post-Soviet experience with poverty and targeting is from the East European one. Overcoming the Soviet legacy has not been as easy as the generally positive East European prototypes would have suggested. Poverty correlates for the FSU are not as sharp or as well-defined as in Eastern Europe, yet poverty levels are also higher in the FSU, presenting a larger challenge to governments as they try to reduce poverty and improve targeting.

We have set ourselves three tasks in this chapter. First, we construct a profile of the incidence and depth of poverty in the six countries, using aggregate poverty indexes. The aim is to find out what the common elements are in the profile of poverty in Eastern Europe and the FSU, and which aspects of poverty are country-specific or bimodal (e.g., the immediate Soviet legacy of the FSU vs. the more diluted Soviet legacy of Eastern Europe). If we find a large common element, it opens up the possibility of a region-wide policy approach to poverty alleviation.

Second, we undertake a multivariate analysis of the determinants of poverty. This overcomes the limitations of the one- or two-dimensional approach typically embodied in a tabular presentation of a poverty profile. Our objective is to find important correlates of poverty, and, where possible, attribute causality to them. The results will also clarify whether the determinants of welfare, such as the demographic characteristics of households and the returns to household assets, differ between the poor and the non-poor.

Our third and most important task is to derive a policy approach toward poverty alleviation. Specifically, we wish to evaluate the role that means testing and indicator-based targeting can play in channeling social transfers to the poor. In part because of the socialist legacy, social transfers constitute a huge component of public expenditure in Eastern Europe and the FSU, representing as much as one-fifth of gross domestic product (GDP). The need to reduce these expenditures is pressing, and the need for suitable targeting devices is high. We will demonstrate the contribution that indicator-based targeting can play.

Each of these three tasks is given a section in this chapter (respectively, Sections 2.3, 2.4, and 2.5). Before presenting empirical results, though, we address in the next section the relevant methodological issues.

## 2.2. METHODOLOGICAL ISSUES IN THE MODELING OF POVERTY

In line with most recent work on poverty, the analysis in this paper is based on a money-metric measure of utility and welfare. Total household expenditure is used as measure of household welfare and as a basis to rank households and to define a poverty line. Expenditure is preferred to income because it is usually reported more accurately in household budget surveys.[1] Furthermore, there is the important theoretical consideration that expenditure reflects better permanent income. This argument is particularly relevant in transition economies where the volatility of current income is still quite high because of the lack of steady private sector employment and the resulting high rates of unemployment. Arrears on the payment of wages and pensions, especially in FSU countries, further adds to the unreliability of current income as a measure of welfare.

The analysis below takes into account differences in needs due to different household size and composition and therefore uses household expenditure per equivalent adult as the welfare measure. There is a wide option of adult equivalency scales, and different scales are used in different countries. Our comparative analysis objectives require the use of a single scale, and we have opted for the OECD scale, because of its simplicity of use and wide familiarity. This scale is expressed as follows

$$EXP_{EQ} = \frac{EXP}{n^{(0.7)}}$$

where $EXP$ is total household expenditure and $n$ is household size.[2] The OECD scale reflects economies of scale regarding household size but does not incorporate gender differences.

Household expenditures were not deflated by a regional price index to take potential differences in prices within the country into account. The reason is that, except for Russia, the countries in the analysis are all fairly small, and regional price differences can be expected to be minor. For example, for Poland (the second-largest country in the set), regional price differences were found not to exceed 2 percent (Grootaert, 1995). For Russia, informal calculations suggested that the effect on poverty estimates of correcting for regional price differences was very small. As discussed in Chapter 1, during the period of analysis, several countries experienced significant inflation, and in these cases expenditures were deflated with a month-by-month consumer price index. This yields real household expenditure per equivalent adult as measure of household welfare.

A cutoff point needs to be selected to serve as poverty line across the distribution of real household expenditure per equivalent adult. We rejected the use of an absolute line, such as $x$ dollars in PPP terms, because of the wide variation in income levels across the six countries. Indeed, it is not very meaningful to compare poverty profiles, when for one country the profile pertains to less than 5 percent of the population and for another country to almost half the population. Hence, we opted for a relative poverty line, which, after some experimentation, was set at two-thirds of mean household expenditure per equivalent adult.[3]

Obviously, the exact position of the poverty line selected affects the results. Individual country studies have shown that in certain ranges of the distribution, even fairly small movements of the poverty line can have large effects on the estimated incidence of poverty (see, e.g., Grootaert, 1995 for Poland; Grootaert, 1997a for Hungary; World Bank, 1995b for Russia). However, poverty profiles tend to be more robust than incidence figures, and significant modifications do not occur unless the poverty line is set in the very lowest ranges of the distribution, especially in the lowest decile. Nevertheless, a sensitivity analysis would be useful, and the earlier cited country studies contain analyses with different poverty lines. The sheer bulk of tabular and regression results for a six-country study make it impractical to include a formal sensitivity analysis in this chapter. We refer the interested reader to the country studies.

Our selection of aggregate poverty index is the popular P-alpha class of poverty measures introduced by Foster, Greer, and Thorbecke (1984). This index is defined as

$$P_\alpha = \frac{1}{n} \sum_{i=1}^{q} \left( \frac{z - y_i}{z} \right)^\alpha$$

where  n  =  number of people
     q  =  number of poor people
     z  =  poverty line
     $y_i$  =  expenditure of individual $i$
     $\alpha$  =  poverty aversion parameter

The poverty aversion parameter can take any positive value or zero. The higher the value the more the index "weighs" the situation of the very poor, the people furthest below the poverty line. Of specific interest are the cases where $\alpha = 0$ and $\alpha = 1$.

If $\alpha = 0$, the index becomes

$$P_0 = \frac{q}{n}$$

which is the simple head count ratio of poverty, that is, the number of poor people as a percentage of the total population. While this is a useful first indicator, it fails to pay attention to the depth of poverty. To do so, one also needs to look at the extent to which the expenditures of poor people fall below the poverty line. This is customarily expressed as the "income gap ratio" or "expenditure gap ratio," which expresses the average shortfall as a fraction of the poverty line itself,

$$\frac{z - \overline{y}_i}{z}$$

where $\overline{y}_i$ is the average income or expenditure of the poor.

A useful index is obtained when the head count ratio of poverty is multiplied with the income or expenditure gap ratio. This corresponds to

$$P_1 = \frac{q}{n} \left( \frac{z - \overline{y}_i}{z} \right)$$

which reflects both the incidence and depth of poverty. This measure has a particularly useful interpretation because it indicates what fraction of the poverty line would have to be contributed by every individual to eradicate poverty through transfers, under the assumption of perfect targeting. This can be considered as the minimal amount of resources needed to eradicate poverty, given that perfect targeting is not likely to be achieved in practice.

In the tables below we show the head count ratio $P_0$, and the ratio $P_1/P_0$, the expenditure gap ratio.[4] We prefer to call the latter "poverty gap" (PG) to highlight that it is a measure of the average depth of poverty calculated over the poor only. In contrast, $P_0$ and $P_1$ are ratios that are calculated over the entire population (for a further discussion of these measures, see Ravallion, 1993). In the tables below each of these measures has been multiplied by 100 for easier interpretation.

The comparative poverty profile in the next section of this paper is based on one- or two-dimensional disaggregations of the P-alpha index. Though this yields a useful identification of important correlates of poverty, it cannot establish the relative importance of each correlate (or determinant, if causality can be assumed). A multivariate model of poverty is hence indicated. A basic model uses real household expenditure per equivalent adult as dependent variable in a regression with exogenous household endowments and characteristics as explanatory variables. Such a welfare model is a reduced-form equation of the various structural equations that express the income-earning and consumption behavior of the household (see, e.g., Glewwe, 1991). This model can explicitly recognize the economic characteristics of the environment in which households operate. Consider the following model:

$$E_i = \beta_1 X_i + \beta_2 W_i + \varepsilon_i \tag{1}$$

where $E_i$ = real household expenditure per equivalent adult of household $i$
$X_i$ = a set of characteristics of households $i$
$W_i$ = a set of characteristics of the economic environment of household $i$
$\beta_{1,2}$ = model parameters
$\varepsilon_i$ = error term

While such a model is not able to predict the effect of household characteristics on specific income or consumption decisions (this would require structural equations), it allows us to observe the net effect of any given characteristic, holding all others constant, on resulting household welfare. It is assumed at this point that there is no simultaneous effect of household welfare on household characteristics so that no $X_i$ are endogenous. This assumption is time-dependent: we assume this to be the case within some relevant time period. (We revisit this issue below when discussing the specific variables to be included in the model). With this assumption, simple Ordinary Least Squares (OLS) estimation of equation (1) is appropriate.

From the point of view of understanding poverty, equation (1) is not optimal. It imposes constant parameters over the entire distribution. It thus assumes that the effect of a given household characteristic, say, education, is the same across the entire welfare spectrum, and that the underlying structural equations do not differ for poor and non-poor. One could say that in this representation the poor are viewed merely as "rich people with less money." This is arguably an incomplete representation. Though one should not, of course, see the poverty line as a barrier that divides the population into two entirely different groups, it is certainly arguable that poor people face different (often severer) constraints in order, say, to obtain credit, to obtain labor market information, to set up enterprises, and so on. On the other hand, they may well be more adept at obtaining transfer income. This calls for additional modeling of poverty.

The most obvious approach might be to estimate the welfare regression separately for poor and non-poor, or introduce a set of interaction variables (between a binary variable for poor/non-poor and the other regressors). Both methods are equivalent econometrically, but their estimation is problematic, because the poverty status variable is clearly endogenous—it is merely a binary representation of the dependent variable. This endogeneity problem also rules out the use of a Heckman-type selection model to, first, determine poverty status and, then, using the derived inverse Mills-ratio to correct the welfare equations of the poor and non-poor groups for selection bias. In practice, since the poverty criterion is the same as the dependent variable in the welfare equations, it would be very difficult to place an identifying restriction on the welfare equation.

A workable solution requires, therefore, that the sample be split on the basis of an exogenous asset that is a good predictor of household welfare or poverty. Existing studies such as those cited earlier in this section and our own results suggest that education would be a prime candidate. Hence, we have split each country sample into four subsamples based on the level of education of the head of household: primary education or less, vocational education, secondary education, and university. This approach is particularly useful because it makes possible an assessment of the way education interacts with other assets of the household and with its demographic characteristics. For example, we can find out whether the returns to owning land or a household enterprise are affected by the level of education. We can also learn whether any welfare gap between male-headed and female-headed households varies with the level of education, and whether the impact of unemployment is severer or less severe for well-educated people.

Quantile regressions are another way to explore differences between poor and rich households. Quantile regressions are a semiparametric method that estimates the regression line through given points on the distribution of the dependent variable (while an OLS regression line goes through the mean). The results can indicate whether certain explanatory factors are weaker or stronger in different parts of the distribution. However, the estimation is conditional upon the values of the independent variables, and hence coefficients from quantile regressions are not comparable with those of OLS regressions.[5]

When estimating poverty models on the basis of household survey data, it needs to be recognized that such data are likely to contain a certain amount of measurement error. If the error is limited to the dependent variable, it does not bias the estimated coefficients (so long as the error is not correlated with any of the regressors), but it will affect the variance-covariance matrix. A potential concern, though, is that the measurement error of household expenditure may rise systematically with the level of expenditure. This increases the probability of correlation with Right-Hand-Side (RHS) variables such as education, which is positively correlated with the level of expenditure. This could lead to biases in the estimation of equation (1).

The presence of measurement error has led several authors to substitute limited-dependent variable models for the continuous welfare equation. Gaiha (1988) used a binary logit model to predict the probability that a rural household in India would be poor.[6] Diamond et al. (1990) estimate a multinomial logit model on U.S. data to predict the probability of belonging to an income quintile, conditional upon certain personal and household characteristics. Diamond et al. justify their approach, relative to a continuous welfare regression, by arguing that the restrictions imposed by the functional form of a levels regression (often linear or log-linear) may cause it to fit poorly on the actual distribution, and they demonstrate that this is the case for their U.S. data set. The multinomial logit model allows for discontinuities in the underlying welfare model and thus also solves the concern of imposing equal parameters over the entire distribution discussed earlier. In the case of two groups (poor and non-poor) the approach collapses to a binary logit or probit model, although then the underlying welfare model is again continuous (Ravallion, 1996). There has been a recent debate in the literature on the merits of welfare regressions versus binary poverty models. Ravallion (1996) argues that the binary response model is redundant, since the parameters measuring the effect of household characteristics on the probability to be poor can be derived from the levels regression, which is consistently estimable under weaker assumptions about the distribution of the error. As argued in Grootaert (1997b), this argument applies if there is only random measurement error and if a case can be made for imposing constant parameters over the entire distribution.

The possibility of systematic measurement error has led us to undertake also probit estimation of a poverty equation where the dependent variable is binary (poor/non-poor). Explanatory variables are the same as in the welfare regression. It is clearly a judgment call whether the loss of information embodied in the binary regression (collapsing the entire distribution into two values) outweighs the risk of bias due to measurement error. However, to the extent that results from a binary model confirm levels-regression results, they can act as a robustness test for the latter. In recent years, use of probit and logit models (mainly the former) have become common practice in poverty analysis (see, e.g., Alderman and Garcia, 1993; Lanjouw and Stern, 1991; World Bank, 1995d, 1996d; Appleton, 1996; Grootaert, 1997b).

In summary, we will estimate the determinants of poverty on the basis of four models:

(i) OLS regression of welfare equation (1).
(ii) Probit estimation of a binary poverty equation. (To address the problem of non-random measurement error, especially mismeasurement as a function of level of expenditure.)

Models iii and iv are used to assess whether returns to assets differ across the welfare distribution:

(iii) Estimation of equation (1) over subsamples defined by the education level of the head of household.
(iv) Quantile regressions at selected points of the household welfare distribution.

Each of these models has the same RHS and we turn now to the discussion of which variables can be considered exogenous household characteristics. As we pointed out earlier, this is mainly a function of the time horizon considered relevant. It has become fashionable in econometrics to take a rather narrow view on this (i.e., to consider a long time horizon) and to estimate welfare models with very parsimonious RHS (see, e.g., Glewwe and Hall, 1995). As Appleton (1995) has argued, reasons can be found why almost every conceivable determinant of poverty is simultaneously determined with welfare, and he cites a number of examples of such discussions in the literature. In the end, little more than gender, age, and a few parental characteristics end up as truly exogenous.[7] Such econometric purity is problematic if the analysis is meant to guide policy. Most policy and targeting variables at the household level become endogenous if the time period is made long enough. All assets (education, physical capital, land) as well as household size are to some degree a function of the household's welfare level and its evolution over the life cycle. Location can change due to migration. Likewise, the household head can change as a result of migration, or one household can split into several households (or the reverse process can occur).

While we recognize the strict validity of these arguments, for this exercise we have taken a pragmatic view, and used a fairly generous set of RHS variables. The objective is to identify determinants of welfare and poverty that, in the short run, are valid policy and targeting variables. As relevant time frame, we consider the reference period for the data collection, which is a year or less. We include therefore on the RHS variables that the typical household in the six transition economies in question cannot change in a one-year period or can change only with great difficulty or cost. This takes the specific situation of these economies into account, and explains, for example, why some labor market variables are included on the RHS. In a fully functioning market economy, occupation and labor market status must be viewed as endogenous, but this is not the case in many transition economies. Unemployment is high and largely structural, retraining opportunities are limited, and in some countries, the supply of housing is not yet sufficiently flexible to permit easy migration to areas of growing labor demand.

On the other hand, among the asset variables, we have not included ownership of durable goods in the RHS for estimating the three models listed above. This is actually more of a judgment call than it may appear. Until a few years ago, in the countries in our analysis, such goods were rationed. With the possible exceptions of Hungary and Estonia, there was not yet a fully operating market for these goods, accessible to the entire population, at the time the surveys underlying the HEIDE data were undertaken. Markets for durable goods such as personal computers and VCRs often existed only in cities, and because of very high relative prices (compared to Western Europe) accumulation and decumulation of such goods was rare for all but the very rich. For many households, the existing stock was still largely determined by the pre-transition allocation. Of course, this situation has been rapidly changing in recent years.

Generally speaking, asset variables have to be seen as endogenous with respect to household welfare, because in an inter-temporal context, the household's welfare level will determine the extent of education children receive and will determine capital accumulation. For one-period model estimation based on cross-sectional household data, the case for exogeneity is stronger but not absolute. In principle, it would be desirable to replace these variables with instruments such as parents' education, inherited wealth, and so on. Unfortunately, such variables are not available in the data sets, and our regressions include productive asset variables on the RHS. In interpreting the regression results, some caution will thus be necessary not to view the estimated coefficients as measuring strictly one-way causality from assets to welfare or poverty.

Using a one-year time frame, we consider as exogenous the following sets of variables:

- household assets: education, physical capital (house, household enterprises), land;
- demographic household characteristics: household size and composition and characteristics of the head of household;
- labor market connections: unemployment, and share of wages in total income;
- economic environment: location.

The *human capital* of the household is embodied in its members and hence their numbers (by sex and age group) are introduced as regressors. Since it is likely that the education of the head of household has a greater influence than that of other members on welfare and poverty outcomes, the education level of the head was introduced as a separate regressor, by means of a series of dummy variables reflecting the highest level of education achieved (primary or less, secondary, vocational/technical, university). The earlier cited country poverty studies have indeed found strong bivariate correlations between poverty incidence and the level of education of the head of household. The data at hand do not provide information on work experience, but this can be proxied by age. The age of the household head is also a good indicator of the stage in the life cycle of the household.

Information on *physical capital* is somewhat scant in the data sets. We know whether the household owns a farm or small business but have no information on the value of its assets. Nevertheless, information on ownership (or use, in countries where legal ownership is still unclear) is bound to be very important because the emergence of small private enterprises is a key feature of transition, and poverty among such entrepreneurs is likely to be below average.

Ownership of a house is important in the same sense. In many cases it provides the location for a household enterprise, and for many households it constitutes the main asset against which they can borrow and from which they derive rental income (actual or imputed). In most transition economies in 1993–1995 (when the HEIDE data were collected), the supply of housing was still quite rigid and a housing market was absent in many locations. Housing ownership was still frequently the result of pre-transition allocations by the state. Hence, there is a strong case for considering homeownership as exogenous to the process of determining welfare. Similarly, ownership of land was not yet a full household choice variable, and, especially in rural areas, it is a key determinant of cash income and consumption of food.

The *link with the labor market* is captured in the model with two variables: the share of wages in total household income, and the number of unemployed household members (in some cases this was replaced by the employment status of the head of household if this variable yielded a better specification). The case for exogeneity of these variables rests on the fact that in the transition context, many of the labor market status outcomes are determined, or at least greatly influenced, by the labor market status that obtained prior to transition or by the macroeconomic changes. Of course, it must be recognized that personal characteristics do contribute to unemployment, or make it more or less likely than a person will successfully obtain self-employment income. Again, instrumental variables would provide a solution if they were available. (One possibility would be to use regional rather than household-specific labor market variables). We kept these variables in the equation mainly because of their importance for targeting, but again recognize the need for caution in interpreting the coefficients.

The way in which the household utilizes its asset endowment is a function of various *demographic household characteristics*. The demographic structure of the household has been shown to have a strong relation with poverty incidence. Beyond the number of children and adults, it is useful to specify the age and gender of the household head because those factors may be related to the household's ability to cope with a changing economic environment.

Last, the incidence of poverty is affected by *the economic environment* in which the household operates. This relates especially to income-earning opportunities and the level of social and economic infrastructure. In a transition context, the household's ability to adjust to a new economic reality will depend very much upon whether it lives in an urban or rural area, in a large or small city, in an old industrial region, and so on. In this research, we will capture this by categorical variables for type of locality (capital or other city, village).[8]

Apart from laying out the set of determinants of welfare and poverty (the objective of Section 2.4), these equations can also be used to investigate how feasible means testing and indicator-based targeting is. Almost all East European and FSU countries rely on these techniques to allocate social assistance and sometimes other transfers as well. If an effective, reliable, and low-cost test for income were available, there would of course be no need for indicator-based targeting. In practice, most social assistance authorities find it very difficult to apply means tests and find that applicants on average underreport income, especially self-employment income. We wanted to test how many poor people could be correctly identified based on a simplified means test and relying on easily identifiable indicators. To that effect we re-estimated equation (1) with an expanded set of variables, adding wage-income and public-transfer income (the two "official" and most easily verifiable income components for most households), and also a list of durable goods owned by the household.

As we discussed earlier, these variables are likely to be endogenous to the level of welfare, but our objective here is simply to predict outcomes. Hence, we do not interpret the estimated coefficients of, say, TV ownership as the "contribution" of this variable to welfare, but merely as a partial correlation coefficient incorporating all feedback effects from welfare to durable ownership. We estimated the expanded equation (1) with forward stepwise OLS, so as to identify the strongest correlates and best predictors first.[9] The results of this exercise are discussed in Section 2.5.

## 2.3. POVERTY PROFILES

The changing nature of poverty in Eastern Europe and the former Soviet Union has paralleled the sharp changes in economic management and in government in the region over the past two decades. Even before the collapse of the Berlin Wall and the breakup of the Soviet Union, East European countries had been experimenting with economic reforms that brought their systems closer to market economies. Two of the early leaders in such reform efforts, Hungary and Poland, are case studies for this analysis. Hungary was arguably the first country in Eastern Europe to embrace economic reforms, with its market-oriented New Economic Mechanism, and Poland's Solidarity movement was an early large-scale populist movement toward more democratic government and a freer economic environment.

Along with economic reform in Eastern Europe quickly came the labor market consequences of shutting down non-profitable state enterprises. Unlike in the FSU, where adjustment was much later and fell almost exclusively on real wages, in Eastern Europe open unemployment along with real wage declines was characteristic of phase changes in government and the economy. One paradoxical result of this is that poverty is much more clearly defined in Eastern Europe than in the FSU, and the poverty profiles of East European countries identify poverty correlates more clearly. This makes improvements in targeting in Eastern Europe much more realistic to posit than in the FSU, where the poor are not so well differentiated from the not-so-poor.

Although this conclusion might seem somewhat surprising, it is not especially new. Even with far more inferior databases, Atkinson and Micklewright (1992) concluded that poverty in Eastern Europe was more defined and less all-encompassing than poverty in the former Soviet Union. However, during the reference period for their work (1991 and earlier) the FSU had not broken up, nor had there been the sharp changes in the macroeconomic environment associated with the dissolution of the FSU, so it is not surprising that the earlier time period and the use of official data led Atkinson and Micklewright (1992) to conclude that overall, FSU poverty was not as severe as in many East European countries and that, further, poverty within the FSU was highly heterogeneous (see also Braithwaite, 1991).

With the breakup of the FSU, there were severe disruptions in the old trading and monetary regimes. The demise of the ruble zone, the political ramifications of the declarations of independence, the buildup of arrears in the payment for energy imports, the difficulties in macromanagement of the newly independent countries, and the difficulties in finding alternative suppliers for intermediate inputs (which in many cases were highly specialized) all combined to result in catastrophic declines in GDP. Whereas the aggregate decline in GDP for the East European countries was 10 percent during the period 1990–1996, it was 45 percent for the FSU. Especially sharp declines were registered in 1993 and 1994, which were runaway-hyperinflation years in most FSU countries.

Under these circumstances, it is hardly surprising that open poverty has increased drastically in the FSU. Poverty also increased in Eastern Europe, but Eastern Europe managed to avoid most of the macroeconomic disruption associated with the breakup of the FSU, or if problems such as hyperinflation and collapsing real wages were encountered, they were encountered much earlier than during 1990–1996. As a result, poverty in Eastern Europe has become much more like poverty in Western Europe—highly correlated with the situation in the formal labor market and the skills of individuals. As the poverty profiles below indicate, in the FSU poverty is not well correlated with the nature of labor market participation of household members, but neither is it well correlated with the lack of formal labor market ties. Basically, in the FSU, poverty is more pervasive than in Eastern Europe and not as well defined. It is much more difficult to differentiate a poor FSU household from a non-poor one based on observable correlates.

These qualitative and quantitative differences in the experience of poverty in Eastern Europe and the FSU are demonstrated by the cross-tabulation of poverty correlates, head counts, and measures of severity of poverty presented below.

## A. Eastern Europe

In Eastern Europe, the start of rapid transition in the early 1990s accelerated the existing trend toward increasing poverty.[10] The main contributing factors were the loss of employment in a suddenly contracting state sector, without coincident emergence of private sector employment. Rapidly rising unemployment has in fact been one of the most visible signs of the social costs of transition. A number of East European countries also experienced significant inflation (although it did not reach the level of the hyperinflation experienced by some FSU countries). Adjustments in wages, pensions, and other social transfers lagged behind, and real incomes for many people fell. However, the emerging evidence suggests that these effects have been fairly short-lived (see Chapter 1). The three East European countries in this study experienced less decline in GDP than did the three FSU countries, and in the 1994–1995 period, they returned to positive growth.

The figures in Table 2.1 indicate that poverty rates as well as poverty gaps are lower in the East European countries than in the FSU countries. As we said in Section 2.2, poverty rates measure the incidence of poverty as the percentage of population below the poverty line (two-thirds of mean household expenditure per equivalent adult); the poverty gap measures the depth of poverty as the poor's average shortfall in expenditures from the poverty line expressed as a percentage of the poverty line. FSU poverty rates exceed 30 percent, and its poverty gaps exceed 20 percent. Russia has the worst situation, with a poverty incidence of almost 40 percent and an average poverty gap of 30 percent. While the poverty rate of Kyrgyz republic is higher (42.5 percent), its poverty gap is lower (25 percent) than Russia's. Hungary and Poland show the most favorable situation, with respective poverty rates of 21 percent and 23 percent. The poverty gap is slightly higher in Hungary (14

**Table 2.1.   Poverty and locality**

| Locality | Bulgaria | Hungary | Poland | Estonia | Kyrgyz republic | Russia |
|---|---|---|---|---|---|---|
| | Head count ($P_0$, in percent) | | | | | |
| Capital | 17.5 | 20.3 | 10.1 | 20.6 | 22.9 | 18.2 |
| Other cities | 20.5 | 17.7 | 16.9 | 31.6 | 38.0 | 38.4 |
| Urban subtotal | 19.9 | 18.5 | 16.2 | 27.5 | 33.3 | 35.8 |
| Rural | 39.2 | 24.0 | 33.8 | 38.7 | 47.2 | 49.6 |
| Total | 26.1 | 20.6 | 23.0 | 30.5 | 42.5 | 39.4 |
| | Poverty gap (in percent) 1/ | | | | | |
| Capital | 19.9 | 13.9 | 13.4 | 19.7 | 24.0 | 20.7 |
| Other cities | 17.8 | 13.5 | 12.7 | 19.2 | 26.2 | 28.7 |
| Urban subtotal | 18.1 | 13.6 | 12.7 | 19.4 | 25.7 | 28.1 |
| Rural | 21.7 | 14.6 | 13.8 | 21.9 | 24.7 | 33.2 |
| Total | 19.8 | 14.1 | 13.3 | 20.2 | 25.0 | 29.8 |

*Note*: 1/ The poverty gap is the poor's average shortfall in expenditures from the poverty line, expressed as a percentage of the poverty line (this measure is also known as the expenditure gap ratio).
*Source*: Household Expenditure and Income Data for Transition Economies data set (HEIDE).

percent) than in Poland (13 percent). It thus appears that poverty in Eastern Europe is much shallower than in FSU, which is good news from the point of view of poverty alleviation in Eastern Europe. It suggests that as economic growth resumes, rising incomes may rapidly lift many people above the poverty line.

## Location

The strong causal role played by changes in employment in creating poverty during transition in Eastern Europe make it likely that transition economies will show strong geographic patterns of poverty and that urban and rural areas will be affected differentially.

This is confirmed by Table 2.1, which shows that in all three East European countries rural poverty is higher than urban poverty. In Bulgaria and Poland, rates of rural poverty incidence are almost twice the urban rates. In Hungary, the urban-rural difference is small. Within urban areas, the differences between the capital and other cities are not so pronounced. (This is a marked difference with the situation in the FSU in which capital cities are markedly less poor than other cities). In Bulgaria and Poland, poverty rates are slightly lower in the capital than in other cities, but in Hungary the reverse is true.

The depth of poverty varies less than the incidence of poverty in Eastern Europe. In general, poverty is slightly deeper in rural areas than in urban areas, but within the latter poverty is deepest in the capital cities. So, while East European capitals have generally less poverty than elsewhere, the poor in those capital cities do have a greater shortfall in expenditure than elsewhere. This situation is distinct from the FSU, where both poverty incidence and poverty gap are lowest in the capital cities.

## Family Composition

Almost all empirical work on poverty in Eastern Europe and the FSU has identified a strong correlation between household size and composition and poverty incidence. In Eastern Europe, the correlation is strongest with number of children. In each of the three countries analyzed here, households with three or more children have poverty incidence about double the national rate (Table 2.2). It does not matter much whether this is a nuclear household or an extended household with more than two adults. The exception is Hungary, where the poverty rate in extended households with three or more children is more than triple the national rate. This is because in Hungary extended households often arise as a result of poverty, which forces separate households to merge in order to benefit from economies of scale in housing and other expenditures.

The implication is that in Eastern Europe, poverty among children is higher than average and that the presence of children needs to be considered as a strong candidate indicator for targeting. We will revisit this proposition in the following sections when reviewing the multivariate results. The finding of a strong correlation between poverty and the presence of children also constitutes a call to reform entitlement programs such as family allowances, which provide fixed

# Table 2.2. Poverty and family composition

| Family composition | Bulgaria | Hungary | Poland | Estonia | Kyrgyz republic | Russia |
|---|---|---|---|---|---|---|
| | **Head count ($P_0$, in percent)** | | | | | |
| One male adult, no children | 33.1 | 24.2 | 15.6 | 32.5 | 40.0 | 52.5 |
| One female adult, no children | 45.0 | 27.8 | 13.5 | 37.0 | 51.8 | 47.8 |
| One adult, one or more children | 23.4 | 32.1 | 28.2 | 43.5 | 39.7 | 45.0 |
| Two adults, no children | 27.4 | 17.9 | 12.2 | 28.2 | 40.1 | 37.4 |
| Two adults, one child | 15.2 | 20.1 | 16.1 | 30.5 | 42.4 | 37.0 |
| Two adults, two children | 19.4 | 19.9 | 24.7 | 29.6 | 39.9 | 38.7 |
| Two adults, three or more children | 61.3 | 38.1 | 43.3 | 28.5 | 49.1 | 64.2 |
| Three or more adults, no children | 22.7 | 13.9 | 16.6 | 24.4 | 37.0 | 30.2 |
| Three or more adults, one child | 20.1 | 17.7 | 20.2 | 27.8 | 35.6 | 35.8 |
| Three or more adults, two children | 35.8 | 29.5 | 36.2 | 31.6 | 43.3 | 51.6 |
| Three or more adults, three or more children | 55.9 | 71.1 | 46.2 | 57.6 | 43.6 | 60.4 |
| All | 26.1 | 20.6 | 23.0 | 30.5 | 42.5 | 39.4 |
| | **Poverty gap (in percent) 1/** | | | | | |
| One male adult, no children | 26.0 | 17.9 | 22.4 | 34.3 | 39.5 | 42.0 |
| One female adult, no children | 28.9 | 18.6 | 17.3 | 27.5 | 47.4 | 44.2 |
| One adult, one or more children | 25.0 | 20.8 | 19.7 | 24.3 | 26.8 | 35.9 |
| Two adults, no children | 20.8 | 13.8 | 14.5 | 20.3 | 31.8 | 33.5 |
| Two adults, one child | 14.3 | 15.1 | 13.6 | 18.8 | 27.7 | 26.9 |
| Two adults, two children | 18.1 | 13.1 | 12.8 | 17.4 | 26.7 | 27.0 |
| Two adults, three or more children | 22.0 | 13.5 | 13.6 | 16.8 | 27.0 | 28.3 |
| Three or more adults, no children | 16.2 | 12.6 | 13.2 | 17.3 | 26.2 | 27.6 |
| Three or more adults, one child | 18.6 | 12.7 | 12.5 | 16.2 | 21.8 | 26.1 |
| Three or more adults, two children | 19.3 | 12.8 | 12.8 | 16.6 | 23.0 | 25.0 |
| Three or more adults, three or more children | 24.5 | 13.8 | 11.7 | 17.1 | 22.8 | 26.6 |
| All | 19.8 | 14.1 | 13.3 | 20.2 | 25.0 | 29.8 |

*Note*: 1/ The poverty gap is the poor's average shortfall in expenditures from the poverty line, expressed as a percentage of the poverty line (this measure is also known as the expenditure gap ratio).
*Source*: Household Expenditure and Income Data for Transition Economies data set (HEIDE).

amounts of money to households with children. These allowances are probably not needed by the richer households, and they are clearly insufficient to prevent households with many children from falling into poverty. A possible solution is to introduce means testing and to increase the amounts given to large poor households. Grootaert (1995, 1997a) contains simulation exercises that demonstrate, in the cases of Poland and Hungary, that this can be achieved in a budget-neutral fashion, and that it has the potential of significantly reducing poverty among children. In part, the potential success from introducing means testing results from the fact that the poverty gap is *not* higher among households with many children. This means that on a per capita basis, the resources needed to lift these households out of poverty is not greater than for other kinds of households. In fact, the uniformity of the poverty gap across different types of households, displayed in Table 2.2, is quite a remarkable feature of poverty in Eastern Europe.

Apart from large households, poverty incidence is also above average in households with one adult. The situation is especially bad among women living alone in Bulgaria, among whom poverty incidence is 45 percent. Most of these are pensioners. In Poland, in contrast, households consisting of one man or one woman have below-average poverty rates, reflecting that pensions in Poland are higher than elsewhere. In Hungary and Poland, one-adult households with children have higher poverty rates than those without children, and there is some evidence that such households are more likely to fall through the cracks of the family allowance system and not receive these benefits (Grootaert, 1995, 1997a). Poor one-adult households also experience deeper poverty than other poor households: in all three countries, they have larger poverty gaps than any other type of households.

While Table 2.2 expresses the composition of the household in terms of the number of adults and the number of children, Table 2.3 indicates that the number of elderly among the adults is also correlated with poverty. Except in Poland, households consisting only of elderly have the highest poverty incidence and poverty gap. We return to this later when discussing the age dimension of poverty.

**Table 2.3.  Poverty and aggregate family composition**

| Family composition | Bulgaria | Hungary | Poland | Estonia | Kyrgyz republic | Russia |
|---|---|---|---|---|---|---|
| | Head count ($P_0$, in percent) | | | | | |
| No children, no elderly | 18.3 | 13.0 | 13.3 | 23.8 | 37.6 | 31.9 |
| Child(ren), no elderly | 25.0 | 23.9 | 28.1 | 32.8 | 43.1 | 40.5 |
| No children, elder(ly), | 39.0 | 26.1 | 18.1 | 39.4 | 43.8 | 43.8 |
| Child(ren), elder(ly) | 28.0 | 22.2 | 32.7 | 35.2 | 42.9 | 51.5 |
| All | 26.1 | 20.6 | 23.0 | 30.5 | 42.5 | 39.4 |
| | Poverty gap (in percent) 1/ | | | | | |
| No children, no elderly | 18.8 | 13.6 | 13.6 | 22.0 | 29.4 | 32.2 |
| Child(ren), no elderly | 19.4 | 14.1 | 13.2 | 18.3 | 24.2 | 27.1 |
| No children, elder(ly) | 21.1 | 15.1 | 15.5 | 22.8 | 34.0 | 35.5 |
| Child(ren), elder(ly) | 19.5 | 10.5 | 11.9 | 19.2 | 23.9 | 27.0 |
| All | 19.8 | 14.1 | 13.3 | 20.2 | 25.0 | 29.8 |

*Note*: 1/ The poverty gap is the poor's average shortfall in expenditures from the poverty line, expressed as a percentage of the poverty line (this measure is also known as the expenditure gap ratio).
*Source*: Household Expenditure and Income Data for Transition Economies data set (HEIDE).

## Labor Force Participation

It is not surprising that labor force status is strongly correlated with poverty outcomes in Eastern Europe. In all countries, wage earners and the self-employed have the lowest poverty incidence and poverty gap (Table 2.4). Which of these two groups does best depends on the stage of transition. In Hungary, with perhaps the best developed private sector, and the earliest initiation of transition, the self-employed have the lowest poverty incidence—slightly more than half the national rate. Elsewhere, though, wage work still provides the better alternative.

Table 2.4 also shows, though, that being a pensioner sharply increases the odds of being poor, except in Poland, and in all countries pensioners have above-average poverty gaps. The favorable situation of pensioners in Poland derives from the generosity of the Polish pension system. Of all East European countries, Poland

**Table 2.4.  Poverty and socioeconomic status**

| Socioeconomic group of household head | Bulgaria | Hungary | Poland | Estonia | Kyrgyz republic | Russia |
|---|---|---|---|---|---|---|
| | Head count ($P_0$, in percent) | | | | | |
| Wage earner | 16.4 | 15.7 | 18.7 | 23.1 | 38.8 | 32.5 |
| Self-employed | 24.3 | 12.7 | 26.8 | 26.7 | 40.3 | 31.5 |
| Pensioner | 44.3 | 27.4 | 19.4 | 47.7 | 57.0 | 52.6 |
| Other transfer recipient | 63.7 | 57.1 | 64.1 | 54.3 | 61.9 | 68.7 |
| Other | 46.5 | 49.4 | 33.5 | 31.0 | 42.2 | 45.2 |
| All | 26.1 | 20.6 | 23.0 | 30.5 | 42.5 | 39.4 |
| | Poverty gap (in percent) 1/ | | | | | |
| Wage earner | 14.4 | 12.1 | 11.7 | 17.0 | 23.4 | 26.9 |
| Self-employed | 15.3 | 11.1 | 14.4 | 24.6 | 24.8 | 27.9 |
| Pensioner | 23.7 | 15.9 | 14.4 | 23.1 | 28.6 | 35.8 |
| Other transfer recipient | 30.0 | 21.1 | 18.6 | 26.1 | 26.8 | 33.1 |
| Other | 28.8 | 16.5 | 11.5 | 17.9 | 25.1 | 27.8 |
| All | 19.8 | 14.1 | 13.3 | 20.2 | 25.0 | 29.8 |

*Note*: 1/ The poverty gap is the poor's average shortfall in expenditures from the poverty line, expressed as a percentage of the poverty line (this measure is also known as the expenditure gap ratio).
*Source*: Household Expenditure and Income Data for Transition Economies data set (HEIDE).

increased spending on pensions the most: between 1988 and 1993, pension spending rose from 6.9 percent to 14.7 percent of GDP (Perraudin and Pujol, 1994). One reason for this was the sudden swelling of the ranks of pensioners by 1.5 million early retirees in the period 1989–1992. Furthermore, in 1992–1993, the average pension in Poland was 64 percent of the average wage—the highest ratio in Eastern Europe. Polish pensions were at that time also fully indexed (Milanovic, 1995).[11]

While the self-employed are a new socioeconomic category in countries in transition, representing people who have succeeded in adapting economically to transition, there is also another socioeconomic category emerging of people who have fallen victim to transition: those who have severed ties to the labor market, and who are unemployed or irregularly employed, and for whom as a result transfer income (other than pensions) has become the main source of income. This category of people has poverty rates that are around 60 percent, and they also have poverty gaps that are above average. However, except for this category of households, Table 2.4 again confirms the remarkable evenness of the poverty gap across society. We already pointed at the uniformity of the poverty gap across demographic types of households (Table 2.2), and the same uniformity is seen across socioeconomic categories.

The specific effect of being unemployed is illustrated in Table 2.5, which shows the poverty measures by the number of unemployed household members. In Hungary, households without unemployed members have a poverty incidence of 16.9 percent. If one household member is unemployed, the figure jumps to 30.5 percent, and it rises further to 68.7 percent if three or more members are unemployed. In Poland, poverty incidence is 19.7 percent in households without an unemployed member but 50.7 percent in households with two unemployed members. Again, though, the poverty gap is not systematically related to the number of unemployed household members, indicating that the social safety net does what it is supposed to do, namely, it prevents the emergence of pockets of deep poverty. (Of course, this finding does not consider overall cost or efficiency in achieving this result).

The role of education in this process is made clear in Table 2.6. There is a distinct difference between the East European and the FSU countries. In Eastern Europe, the link between lower poverty and higher education is extremely pronounced, but in the FSU this link is much weaker, to being almost non-existent in the Kyrgyz republic. In Hungary, for example, the poverty incidence among households where the head has primary education or less is 33.9 percent, while in households where the head has university education, it is 3.3 percent—ten times less. The equivalent figures for the Kyrgyz republic are 43.2 percent and 37.6 percent. The other countries are somewhere between these extremes.

This difference in the impact of education is clearly related to the stage of transition. The further advanced transition is, the more a private sector emerges that needs well-educated workers with general education backgrounds, which makes them flexible and adapt-

## Table 2.5. Poverty and unemployment

| Number of unemployed members in the household | Bulgaria | Hungary | Poland | Estonia | Kyrgyz republic | Russia |
|---|---|---|---|---|---|---|
| | Head count ($P_0$, in percent) | | | | | |
| 0 | ... | 16.9 | 19.7 | 28.4 | 42.0 | 37.6 |
| 1 | ... | 30.5 | 35.7 | 42.6 | 41.9 | 53.2 |
| 2 | ... | 39.2 | 50.7 | 53.1 | 54.4 | 73.7 |
| 3 or more | ... | 68.7 | 46.5 | 73.2 | 40.6 | 66.7 |
| All | 26.1 | 20.6 | 23.0 | 30.5 | 42.5 | 39.4 |
| | Poverty gap (in percent) 1/ | | | | | |
| 0 | ... | 13.1 | 13.0 | 19.5 | 24.4 | 30.1 |
| 1 | ... | 16.0 | 13.6 | 22.2 | 26.5 | 28.5 |
| 2 | ... | 13.6 | 15.1 | 27.3 | 24.4 | 25.6 |
| 3 or more | ... | 17.9 | 17.5 | 30.8 | 33.9 | 39.7 |
| All | 19.8 | 14.1 | 13.3 | 20.2 | 25.0 | 29.8 |

*Note*: 1/ The poverty gap is the poor's average shortfall in expenditures from the poverty line, expressed as a percentage of the poverty line (this measure is also known as the expenditure gap ratio).
*Source*: Household Expenditure and Income Data for Transition Economies data set (HEIDE).

able to the newly emerging skill requirements. Pre-transition vocational and technical education, often geared toward traditional industrial occupations, is no longer in demand. Similarly, low-skill jobs, of the type held by workers with primary education or less, have disappeared in great numbers. The more advanced transition countries such as Hungary and Poland have already experienced skill shortages in fields like engineering, computer science and the like, and this will further push up wages received by workers with university education, and increase the wage gap across skill levels. This is one of the main reasons why the distribution of wages has increased in many transition economies (Milanovic, 1995, 1997).

Education is also the only dimension where the poverty gap is *not* uniform across categories in Eastern Europe. Workers with primary or less education have not only poverty rates well above average, but the poverty gap is also significantly higher than for other groups. Households where the head has a university education have

**Table 2.6.  Poverty and education**

| Education of household head | Bulgaria | Hungary | Poland | Estonia | Kyrgyz republic | Russia |
|---|---|---|---|---|---|---|
| | Head count ($P_0$, in percent) | | | | | |
| Primary or less | 41.1 | 33.9 | 33.0 | 41.5 | 43.2 | 46.2 |
| Secondary | 15.6 | 10.4 | 13.1 | 30.0 | 49.2 | 40.3 |
| Vocational/technical 1/ | 15.0 | 18.7 | 26.3 | ... | 41.3 | 39.5 |
| University or above | 8.9 | 3.3 | 3.8 | 12.7 | 37.6 | 25.9 |
| All | 26.1 | 20.6 | 23.0 | 30.5 | 42.5 | 39.4 |
| | Poverty gap (in percent) 2/ | | | | | |
| Primary or less | 21.6 | 15.6 | 14.7 | 22.7 | 35.4 | 35.4 |
| Secondary | 16.1 | 11.8 | 12.8 | 19.4 | 29.6 | 29.6 |
| Vocational/technical 1/ | 12.6 | 11.9 | 12.3 | ... | 28.2 | 28.2 |
| University or above | 14.6 | 9.8 | 8.1 | 14.8 | 24.0 | 24.0 |
| All | 19.8 | 14.1 | 13.3 | 20.2 | 29.8 | 29.8 |

*Note*: 1/ For Estonia, secondary education and vocational-technical education are combined and shown in the category labeled "Secondary." Definitional problems in the Estonian data set precluded a separation of these two kinds of education.

2/ The poverty gap is the poor's average shortfall in expenditures from the poverty line, expressed as a percentage of the poverty line (this measure is also known as the expenditure gap ratio).

*Source*: Household Expenditure and Income Data for Transition Economies data set (HEIDE).

the lowest poverty gap of any category, along any dimension, displayed in the poverty profile. It may be surprising that the poverty gap varies so much with education level, while it varies very little with the number of unemployed in the household. In part, the reason is that education is not used as a targeting variable for any transfer program (although our results suggest that perhaps it should become a targeting variable for Eastern Europe—see Section 2.5). Although clearly low education is in itself a contributing factor to unemployment, many people with low education still hold full-time jobs (let us not forget that they are a very large category: in Poland and Hungary, about two-thirds of households have heads with primary or vocational/technical education). Their wages are low, and as our results indicate, often insufficient to keep them above the poverty line. Still, as full-time workers, they do not qualify for any transfers (other than general entitlements) to supplement their income. There is no immediate solution to this situation. In the medium to long term, retraining and a general upgrading of schooling curricula will reduce the number of people with low education. Also, people with low education are older than average, and many of them will become absorbed in the pension system in the near term. Whether this will alleviate their poverty depends partly upon policies pertaining to minimum pensions.

## Gender and Age

We already noted the correlation between household composition and poverty outcomes, especially the association between the presence of three or more children and high poverty incidence. Since demographic household characteristics are easily observable and potentially useful targeting variables, it is worthwhile to look in more detail at the age and gender dimensions of poverty in Eastern Europe.

Table 2.7 shows that female-headed households have systematically higher poverty incidence and poverty gaps than do male-headed households. The difference is slight in Poland, but more pronounced in Hungary and Bulgaria. The multivariate analysis in the next section will confirm that such a gender effect remains even after controlling for the characteristics of female-headed households that are strongly correlated with poverty, such as low education.

The age distribution of poverty in Table 2.8 highlights the extent to which poverty in Eastern Europe is concentrated among the very young and the very old. The average poverty incidence in Poland is 23 percent, but among children under ten it exceeds 30 percent. The numbers for Hungary show a similar pattern. In Bulgaria, the relative concentration of poverty among children is actually least. This is not a contradiction with the earlier finding that in Bulgaria poverty rates among households with three or more children are very high, because such households are quite rare in Bulgaria (much rarer than in the other two countries). Hence, in Bulgaria most children live in households with one or two children where poverty rates are lower.

Poverty incidence in Eastern Europe decreases with age, and

**Table 2.7.    Poverty and gender of household head**

| Gender of household head | Bulgaria | Hungary | Poland | Estonia | Kyrgyz republic | Russia |
|---|---|---|---|---|---|---|
| | Head count ($P_0$, in percent) | | | | | |
| Male | 24.0 | 19.1 | 22.7 | 27.9 | 41.6 | 37.8 |
| Female | 40.5 | 25.6 | 23.7 | 39.1 | 50.5 | 46.0 |
| All | 26.1 | 20.6 | 23.0 | 30.5 | 42.5 | 39.4 |
| | Poverty gap (in percent) 1/ | | | | | |
| Male | 18.6 | 13.3 | 13.0 | 18.7 | 24.7 | 28.5 |
| Female | 24.5 | 16.0 | 14.2 | 23.9 | 27.5 | 34.5 |
| All | 19.8 | 14.1 | 13.3 | 20.2 | 25.0 | 29.8 |

*Note*: 1/ The poverty gap is the poor's average shortfall in expenditures from the poverty line, expressed as a percentage of the poverty line (this measure is also known as the expenditure gap ratio).
*Source*: Household Expenditure and Income Data for Transition Economies data set (HEIDE).

reaches a minimum at ages 35–44 in Bulgaria, ages 45–54 in Hungary, and ages 55–64 in Poland. After those ages, the increase in poverty incidence is quite rapid and severe, except in Poland (thanks, as we noted earlier, to the generous pension system in Poland). In Bulgaria and Hungary, poverty rates among people over 75 are close to twice the national average. The vast majority of people in that age group are women, and their poverty rates are higher than for the men in that group. Actually, the gender breakdown of Table 2.8 (not shown here) reveals that poverty rates among the elderly are higher for women in general than for men. At lower ages, though, the gender gap is not very pronounced, and for some ages poverty is lower among women than men.

Gender is thus a relevant poverty dimension in Eastern Europe primarily for the elderly, especially at very high ages, and for female-headed households. For many women, the labor market changes of transition have had major implications. Prior to transition, women were expected to work full time, but the state provided day care for their children. Transition has led to a drop in female labor force participation (not all of it voluntary), but it has also led to a reduced

**Table 2.8. Poverty and age**

| Age bracket | Bulgaria | Hungary | Poland | Estonia | Kyrgyz republic | Russia |
|---|---|---|---|---|---|---|
| | | | **Head count ($P_0$, in percent)** | | | |
| 0–4 | 29.0 | 30.0 | 35.3 | 33.3 | 46.4 | 47.9 |
| 5–9 | 28.2 | 26.0 | 31.6 | 32.0 | 46.0 | 42.9 |
| 10–14 | 24.2 | 20.9 | 27.6 | 34.1 | 41.1 | 40.5 |
| 15–24 | 24.1 | 19.7 | 23.6 | 26.4 | 41.8 | 36.6 |
| 25–34 | 23.5 | 21.7 | 26.2 | 27.6 | 43.3 | 41.6 |
| 35–44 | 18.8 | 17.1 | 21.3 | 28.6 | 38.2 | 34.7 |
| 45–54 | 20.2 | 13.7 | 16.0 | 24.1 | 35.2 | 29.7 |
| 55–64 | 27.6 | 15.6 | 14.5 | 31.6 | 42.6 | 41.7 |
| 65–74 | 35.0 | 23.6 | 18.3 | 37.0 | 47.6 | 45.0 |
| 75 & over | 47.5 | 37.7 | 22.1 | 47.9 | 41.4 | 45.9 |
| All | 26.1 | 20.6 | 23.0 | 30.5 | 42.5 | 39.4 |
| | | | **Poverty gap (in percent) 1/** | | | |
| 0–4 | 21.2 | 14.8 | 14.2 | 20.4 | 24.9 | 29.6 |
| 5–9 | 18.7 | 13.6 | 12.9 | 17.6 | 24.8 | 27.5 |
| 10–14 | 19.5 | 13.2 | 12.4 | 18.6 | 23.6 | 25.9 |
| 15–24 | 18.7 | 14.1 | 12.8 | 18.5 | 24.1 | 28.4 |
| 25–34 | 20.1 | 13.6 | 13.5 | 20.3 | 25.8 | 28.0 |
| 35–44 | 17.7 | 13.5 | 12.6 | 18.7 | 24.1 | 27.6 |
| 45–54 | 17.0 | 12.9 | 13.6 | 20.8 | 24.8 | 30.0 |
| 55–64 | 19.2 | 13.9 | 14.5 | 21.4 | 26.1 | 32.5 |
| 65–74 | 20.6 | 14.4 | 14.2 | 22.0 | 28.5 | 35.2 |
| 75 & over | 26.1 | 17.4 | 15.4 | 26.0 | 34.2 | 37.7 |
| All | 19.8 | 14.1 | 13.3 | 20.2 | 25.0 | 29.8 |

*Note*: 1/ The poverty gap is the poor's average shortfall in expenditures from the poverty line, expressed as a percentage of the poverty line (this measure is also known as the expenditure gap ratio).
*Source*: Household Expenditure and Income Data for Transition Economies data set (HEIDE).

supply of affordable day-care centers (World Bank, 1996e).[12] Both factors may well affect female-headed households disproportionately.

Nevertheless, the poverty figures suggest that in general the age-effect outweighs the gender-effect. This is clear also from Table 2.9, which classifies households by the number of elderly people (over

**Table 2.9.  Poverty and the elderly**

| Number of elderly members (over age 65) in the household | Bulgaria | Hungary | Poland | Estonia | Kyrgyz republic | Russia |
|---|---|---|---|---|---|---|
| | **Head count ($P_0$, in percent)** | | | | | |
| 0 | 21.9 | 19.5 | 22.8 | 28.5 | 42.1 | 37.3 |
| 1 | 33.9 | 23.7 | 24.1 | 39.1 | 45.0 | 47.4 |
| 2 | 38.2 | 27.6 | 22.3 | 36.4 | 39.4 | 42.4 |
| 3 or more | ... | 56.8 | 24.7 | ... | ... | 50.0 |
| All | 26.1 | 20.6 | 23.0 | 30.5 | 42.5 | 39.4 |
| | **Poverty gap (in percent) 1/** | | | | | |
| 0 | 19.1 | 13.9 | 13.3 | 19.6 | 25.0 | 28.8 |
| 1 | 22.2 | 15.2 | 13.5 | 23.6 | 24.3 | 32.7 |
| 2 | 18.5 | 13.7 | 13.2 | 17.5 | 29.2 | 32.1 |
| 3 or more | ... | 7.4 | 13.9 | ... | ... | 58.4 |
| All | 19.8 | 14.1 | 13.3 | 20.2 | 25.0 | 29.8 |

*Note*: 1/ The poverty gap is the poor's average shortfall in expenditures from the poverty line, expressed as a percentage of the poverty line (this measure is also known as the expenditure gap ratio).
*Source*: Household Expenditure and Income Data for Transition Economies data set (HEIDE).

65) in the household. In Bulgaria and Hungary, households without elderly members have below average poverty rates and those with elderly members have above average poverty incidence. The latter increases with the number of elderly. Poland is again the exception, where age proves to be an irrelevant dimension of poverty. As discussed previously, Poland's pension system should be credited with this result.

The poverty gap shows little variation by age, although it is above average among people over age 65. It does not, however, increase systematically with the number of elderly in a household. In fact, in Hungary, the reverse occurs—the poverty gap falls significantly in households with two or three elderly members. Many such households are poor, but they are not very far below the poverty line.

## B. Former Soviet Union

Poverty in the FSU was hidden and unacknowledged, but it was a fact of life for approximately 6–10 percent of the population before the breakup of the country and the embarkation on transitions to the market economy by the FSU countries (Braithwaite, 1990, 1991, 1995). Five years after gaining or regaining independence, poverty has become much more overt and has increased in scope. The large increases in measured poverty have three major causes: severe macroeconomic declines, including hyperinflation; sharp increases in income inequality; and measurement error, especially regarding the actual distribution of real consumption in the pre-transition period.

Any comparison to the pre-transition period is fraught with methodological pitfalls. Even the extent of macroeconomic declines is difficult to assess (Koen and Gavrilenko, 1994), although virtually no one would disagree that the FSU countries experienced especially sharp contractions in output starting in 1992. The hyperinflations experienced in 1993–1994 by most FSU countries meant that the real value of wages, pensions, and other cash transfers plummeted abruptly. The hyperinflations and the breakup of the ruble zone led to macroeconomic disruption and a breakdown of the external trading relationships among the FSU. Without reasonable trading regimes and owing to the necessity for a complete realignment of production, real output declined precipitously.

At the same time that the size of the pie shrank, its distribution became markedly more unequal. The only statistics available are based on income and on the family budget surveys, which are characterized by marked methodological shortcomings. Nonetheless, even a casual comparison suggests that the extent of open income inequality has become quite large during the transition (Klugman and Braithwaite, 1998; Koen, 1996; Commander, Tolstopiatenko, and Yemtsov, 1997).

A further complication stems from the prevalence of arrears in wages and pensions in the FSU countries, and the irregular nature of even formal state-sector employment due to forced administrative leave without pay and reduced working hours. Since the breakup of the FSU, wage and cash transfer arrears have become common as countries have grappled with the introduction of stabilization programs and fiscal austerity. Budgetary sequestration in Russia, Armenia, and the Kyrgyz republic resulted in long delays for wages in the "budgetary sphere" (health, education, government/administration, the Armed Forces, law enforcement, etc.) and for cash transfers, including pensions and child allowances.

It is difficult to accurately measure "official" or "registered" income given the prevalence of arrears, but it is practically impossible to quantify the informal sector in transition economies. In the FSU countries, households have been extremely reluctant to report most of their income even to survey researchers, much less to the tax authorities (Koen and Gavrilenko, 1994). Most studies suggest that the informal sector is around 40 percent of official GDP (Kaufmann and Kaliberda, 1996). In this study, total reported household income as a percent of total household expenditures varied from less than 50 percent in the Kyrgyz republic to more than 95 percent in Estonia. However, the difference between reported income and household expenditures is large enough to mean that conclusions about the distribution of consumption inferred from the distribution of income are problematic. This is one of the reasons why the poverty profile in this study is based on household expenditures.

It is also futile to compare exactly the distribution of consumption before and after transition. During the pre-transition period, wages and prices were controlled, and food and other consumer goods were allocated by queuing, rationing, and favoritism. Neither money income nor money expenditure reflected adequately the household's real consumption, since much of that real consumption was allocated to the household through non-market, non-money means. For example, senior workers at larger enterprises received better housing than junior workers at smaller enterprises, and they had shorter queues for purchasing automobiles. Without ever considering their money income, senior workers were better off. Unfortunately, there is no reliable way to reconstruct the real consumption of the poor and non-poor prior to transition because of the absence of reliable, non-biased household data sets.

Our analysis of post-transition data indicates that the working poor predominate in the poverty profile of the FSU countries. By and large, in Estonia, Russia, and the Kyrgyz republic, the head of household of poor families is employed, most often in the state sector. Results indicate that poverty rates in rural areas are much higher than in urban areas.

## Location

In most countries, where a family lives has a significant correlation with poverty. In the FSU and particularly Russia, there is a strong regional component to poverty, relating to the legacy of the planned economy. There are many one-company towns in the FSU that produced military-industrial goods for which demand has either disappeared or sharply declined. Russia has its "rust belt" where textile production has been displaced by competition from cheaper imports, and service or other industry has not developed to fill in this gap. Additionally, the quality, irrigation, and altitude of agricultural land varies, which means that rural poverty is not homogeneous.

In all the countries compared in this chapter, urban poverty is markedly lower than rural poverty, and the poverty rate in the capital city is the lowest (except in Hungary, Table 2.1). For the East European countries, this is a conventional finding. In many countries of the world, the rural poverty rate is higher than the urban poverty rate, and the higher living standards of urban regions were portrayed as the major explanation for rural-urban migration many years ago (Harris and Todaro, 1970). However conventional this finding may be for Eastern Europe, it is not standard for the FSU. In almost every World Bank poverty assessment completed to date for FSU countries, rural poverty has been found to be somewhat less or markedly less severe than urban poverty both in terms of the head count and in terms of various measures of severity.[13]

The HEIDE data set may lead to different conclusions for two reasons. First, conditions in the transition countries may have changed from the time period referenced by the Poverty Assessments and that covered by the HEIDE database. Second, as described in the methodological section, the HEIDE database uses an equivalent adult approach (which was not usually followed in Poverty Assessments), a relative poverty line, and relied on self-reporting for the value of food produced by the household for its own consumption. In most of the World Bank's poverty assessments for the FSU, the value of food produced on private plots was imputed, usually based on the purchase prices reported by all the households in the sample. Imputing the value of food this way tends to lead to a higher consumption aggregate than asking respondents to assess the market value of their food production.

In Estonia, there is little difference between the depth of poverty in Talinn, the capital, in other cities, or in rural areas as measured by the poverty gap. In the Kyrgyz republic, the average poverty gap seems to be most affected by the higher poverty gap in other cities, since there is little difference between the poverty rate in the capital and the countryside. In Russia, the poverty gap is highest in rural areas and noticeably lower in the capital.

## Family Composition

It is a truism of poverty studies that family composition is one of the most significant correlates of poverty, since the number of earners and dependents has a critical impact on the family's consumption needs and ability to fulfill those needs. In the FSU, however, family composition does not correlate as strongly with poverty as it does in Eastern Europe or in many other countries of the world (Tables 2.2 and 2.3). For example, consider the issue of children. In this study, children were defined to be under the age of 15, which corresponds to the statistical definition of labor activity previously used in the FSU, where those ages 0–14 were assumed to be outside of the "available labor resources" of the country.[14]

In most poor countries, families with children are worse off than families without children, and families with more children are worse off than families with few children. The first part of this generalization seems to apply only weakly to the FSU countries in terms of poverty rates, while the latter part seems to be clearly demonstrated in Estonia and Russia, but to a lesser extent in the Kyrgyz republic. Considering aggregated family composition, in all three countries, families without children and without elderly members are less likely (the Kyrgyz republic) or much less likely (Estonia, Russia) to be poor than families with either. In Russia and Estonia, the highest poverty rates were experienced by families with both children and elderly members (52 and 35 percent, respectively). The Kyrgyz republic showed the lowest degree of variation of poverty rates according to family composition.

These findings are influenced by the overall demographic characteristics of the populations compared. The Russian and Estonian populations are much older than the Kyrgyz republic's, and the birthrate in Estonia is even lower than that in Russia, which is itself very much lower than the birthrate in the Kyrgyz republic. The relative youth of the Kyrgyz population and the widespread prevalence of children means that very few Kyrgyz households are without at least one young dependent (14.4 percent), while nearly half of families in Estonia (49.5) and Russia (44.5) do not have a child.

In Estonia, families with three adults and three children, single-parent families with one or more children, and single female adults have the highest poverty rates, but poverty is most severe for single persons living alone. In Estonia, the dependency burden is more associated with care of the elderly than with children. Families with children constituted only 53 percent of the poor, and families with two adults and any number of children had a lower poverty rate than average. In contrast, families with one or two elderly members were poorer than average. About 18 percent of the poor are age 65 or above, and given the differential male-female survival, approximately three-quarters of the elderly poor are female (Table 2.8).

In Russia, out of all poor individuals, approximately 60 percent live in families with children, while slightly more than 40 percent live in childless homes. However, the poverty rates and gaps are higher for single-person households than in single-parent households and significantly higher than two-adult households with one or two children. This is an unusual finding, and the fact that one of the highest poverty rates recorded was for a single-male adult family type is even more surprising. One would expect that a single male adult would have no dependents and presumably would have a reasonable earnings potential. Age only partly explains this finding, since two-thirds of these single male adults are *younger* than 65. For single Russian females, the poverty rate was high, but so too was the share (60 percent) age 65 or older.

Other findings for Russia are more conventional. Families with three or more children have the highest poverty rate in the sample (but not the highest poverty gap). Families without an elderly member (age 65 or above) have a much lower rate than families with one or two elderly members. In Russia, more of the poor have children than are responsible for an elderly member. However, those families with elderly members have a higher poverty gap than families with children.

In the Kyrgyz republic, a single female living alone was the household type with the highest poverty rate and gap, followed by a many-child household with only two adult members. This is probably related to the situation of the elderly, who do not constitute as high a share of the poor or total population because of the younger age structure of the population. Additionally, in the Kyrgyz republic, having a child is fairly universal—only 14 percent of all families or of poor families do not have at least one child.

Even though most families with two or three children are not poor, there are so many such families in the Kyrgyz republic that they constitute the clear majority of the poor: families with three or more children make up 53 percent of the poor, while families with two or more children are 72 percent of the poor. Such families are less likely to be severely poor, though, as their poverty gaps are lower than those of single females or males, or interestingly enough, of two adults without children.

## Labor Force Participation

Aside from the truism that the more income earners in a household, the better off the household is, there are some unexpected differences about the relationship between labor force participation and poverty in the FSU transition economies relative to other countries. The first difference is that in the FSU, participating in the labor force does not always mean that the participant is paid anything at all. Due to the pervasive wage and cash transfer arrears (notably for pensions, but also for child allowances), the notion "working poor" takes on a whole different meaning. Indeed, there are many who are working poor but would not be poor if their salaries were paid, and there are pensioners that would not be poor if their transfer payments were received on time.

In 1997, Russia announced a commitment to clear pension arrears by the end of the year. Previously, and during the survey period studied here, pension arrears were averaging anywhere between three and nine months, with some more remote areas having much longer lags in payment than in the well-off areas such as Moscow and St. Petersburg. On the other end of the spectrum, Estonia initiated a pension reform in 1993 that reduced differentiated pensions, eliminated pension payment arrears, and provided for gradual increases in the retirement age.

In addition to arrears, the phenomenon of retaining workers by forcing them to work reduced hours (short time) or to be on unpaid administrative leave (forced leave) was widespread in Russia and the Kyrgyz republic.

A second difference between the transition economies of the FSU and other developing economies is that the stigma of reporting that one is out of work is arguably greater, while the entitlement attitude that one deserves a pension or allowance is perhaps larger than in other country contexts. This is due to the legacy of the previous system, in which labor was perceived as the right and obligation of anyone who was able-bodied, but that those who had contributed previously to the labor market would be protected in old age or during periods of temporary "disability" (e.g., pregnancy or illness). These attitudes are likely to evoke positive answers to survey questions such as "Do you work?" or "Do you have a job?" in conditions that might receive negative answers in other countries. Nonetheless, unemployment rates calculated from the HEIDE data are higher than both registered unemployment in the FSU and the rate of unemployment benefit receipts reported by HEIDE respondents, reflecting the extreme difficulty of qualifying for an unemployment benefit and its short duration, especially in Russia and the Kyrgyz republic.

A third particular aspect of the labor market in the transition economies of the FSU is that it is extremely in flux, as the private sector emerges, and the informal labor market offers almost as many opportunities at the top end of the scale as it does at the bottom. Given the historic legacy in Russia and the other FSU countries, where entrepreneurial behavior has always been regarded with extreme distrust, it is truly difficult to determine the extent of entrepreneurial business and earnings. As a result, the number of respondents who report that they work in the private sector might be understated. It might be preferable for a person who has a state sector job "in name only" to maintain that legal affiliation while in essence running a full-time business on the side.

With these caveats in mind, the conclusions about poverty and labor market participation for the FSU countries are rather conventional (Tables 2.4 and 2.5). Households with employed heads have lower poverty rates than those with unemployed heads, while the addition of one or two household members who are unemployed sharply increases the poverty rate. In Estonia, a third unemployed member increases the poverty rate further, but this is not the case in Russia and in the Kyrgyz republic, perhaps for some of the reasons detailed above. However, all three countries demonstrated an increasing poverty gap with each additional unemployed household member.

Some occupations or socioeconomic groups are associated with a lower poverty rate than others. In all three countries, self-employed household heads live in households with a lower poverty rate than average, as do heads who describe themselves as wage earners. However, those self-employed heads who are poor are poorer than average in Estonia. In all three countries, wage earners live in households with a lower poverty gap. Households with pensioners and other transfer recipients as household heads have sharply higher poverty rates than average, but their average shortfall in expenditures is not markedly different from average.

In Estonia and the Kyrgyz republic, households with access to land—a private plot—had lower poverty rates than households without land, and the poverty gap was smaller (Table 2.10). Unlike other studies of Russia (Klugman, 1997; World Bank, 1995b; Kolev, 1996), this study found that Russian households with a plot were

**Table 2.10.  Poverty and ownership of a private plot**

| Whether the household has a private plot | Bulgaria | Hungary | Poland | Estonia | Kyrgyz republic | Russia |
|---|---|---|---|---|---|---|
| **Head count ($P_0$, in percent)** | | | | | | |
| No plot | 26.6 | ... | 18.5 | 34.4 | 48.2 | 38.1 |
| Has plot | 25.6 | ... | 26.5 | 27.7 | 39.1 | 43.5 |
| All | 26.1 | 20.6 | 23.0 | 30.5 | 42.5 | 39.4 |
| **Poverty gap (in percent) 1/** | | | | | | |
| No plot | 21.6 | ... | 13.6 | 21.4 | 28.1 | 29.1 |
| Has plot | 17.2 | ... | 13.2 | 19.2 | 22.2 | 31.8 |
| All | 19.8 | 14.1 | 13.3 | 20.2 | 25.0 | 29.8 |

*Note*: 1/ The poverty gap is the poor's average shortfall in expenditures from the poverty line, expressed as a percentage of the poverty line (this measure is also known as the expenditure gap ratio).
*Source*: Household Expenditure and Income Data for Transition Economies data set (HEIDE).

poorer than households without. As noted above, the change in methodology from imputing the value of private plot produce to relying on self-valuation may explain partially why this result was obtained.

Education of the household head has a strong influence on the household's poverty status, with the lowest head counts achieved by those with a university education (Table 2.6). In all three countries, households headed by those with primary education or less than complete primary education had poverty rates higher than average, and higher than those with secondary education. The depth of poverty paralleled the poverty rates, with the highest poverty gaps for those with primary or less education, followed by secondary and vocational-technical education. The poverty gaps for those poor with higher education were below average.

## Gender

Unlike most of the World Bank's poverty assessments, this study suggests that gender is a significant dimension of poverty (Table 2.7) in the FSU. In the three FSU countries, the poverty rate was sharply higher in households headed by women, with this difference being largest in Estonia and smallest in the Kyrgyz republic. Additionally, female-headed households were poorer than comparable male-headed households as their poverty gaps were larger, although this difference was not as pronounced as the difference in poverty rates.

Given the differential survival rates of women and men, for all three countries, women comprise an increasing share of those who are poor as age increases. Half or even fewer than half of poor children are girls, but by age 65 and over, women are approximately 70–75 percent of the poor. The elderly age 65 and above are also poorer than average, as measured by the poverty gap. This means that elderly female poverty is more pervasive as well as deeper than male poverty in the former Soviet Union.

## 2.4. MULTIVARIATE ANALYSIS OF WELFARE AND POVERTY

The goal of the multivariate analysis of welfare and poverty is to assess the relative importance of various correlates of poverty and, if possible, to attribute causality to these correlates. Additionally, determinants of welfare such as the demographic characteristics of households and the return to household assets may differ between the poor and the non-poor, and the multivariate analysis will help to elucidate these differences. As was the case with the two-dimensional examination of poverty in the poverty cross-tabulation tables, by and large these goals were better met by results for the East European countries. Almost all the variables included in the models for the East European countries have estimated parameters significantly different from zero, and the pattern of results is very consistent across the three East European countries. Thus, while there remain important unidentified welfare determinants (e.g., personal ability), the model does point at a set of significant factors that affect welfare outcomes and that can be identified and affected in the context of policy intervention to alleviate poverty in Eastern Europe.

Unfortunately, the results are not so clear for the FSU. Overall, the explanatory power of the welfare regressions is low, and it is difficult to find as many clear poverty correlates as for the East European countries. In several ways, it can be argued that such a finding is not surprising, and relates to the different degrees of the transition process. In particular, the FSU still had little open unemployment during the HEIDE survey periods, although there was a strong correlation between actual unemployment and poverty. Further, in the FSU the labor market and especially the private sector are not well defined, and it is difficult to determine a priori who are likely to be the losers and winners, since many of the traits associated with winning in the new regimes (entrepreneurial skills, political connections) are extremely difficult to measure reliably by a household survey. However, those aspects that could be measured in the household surveys (access to a household business or private plot) were strongly associated with the ability of a household to avoid poverty in the FSU.

## A.  Eastern Europe

### Welfare Equations

Several general observations emerge from the estimation results in Table 2.11. While moderate, the overall goodness of fit is in line with typical results for this type of equation ($R^2$ ranges from 0.267 to 0.301). The reported results are for the log-linear functional form. These were compared against the results from the linear form, using the test developed for that purpose by Davidson and MacKinnon (1981). In each case the test results pointed at the superiority of the log-linear specification. This implies that effects of household characteristics on welfare are proportional rather than linear. For example, the effect of education is to increase expenditure per equivalent adult in a fixed proportion, rather than with a fixed amount (i.e., the absolute returns are lower for the poor).

The general pattern of findings is that education and the ownership of a household enterprise have the largest effects on welfare outcomes, followed by the nature of the household's link with the labor market. Demographic characteristics are a distant third. Some coun-

**Table 2.11.** **Welfare equations (OLS): East European countries Dependent variable = ln (household expenditure per equivalent adult)**

| | Bulgaria | | Hungary | | Poland | |
|---|---|---|---|---|---|---|
| | Parameter estimate | Standard error | Parameter estimate | Standard error | Parameter estimate | Standard error |
| Intercept | 8.558* | 0.122 | 9.424* | 0.042 | 7.556* | 0.036 |
| Number of children | −0.064* | 0.013 | −0.075* | 0.005 | −0.091* | 0.003 |
| Number of male adults | −0.065* | 0.015 | −0.012 | 0.007 | −0.022* | 0.005 |
| Number of female adults | −0.039* | 0.014 | −0.011 | 0.007 | −0.017* | 0.005 |
| Number of elderly | −0.084* | 0.020 | −0.039* | 0.010 | −0.025* | 0.007 |
| Education of head: primary | −0.235* | 0.024 | −0.228* | 0.011 | −0.195* | 0.008 |
| Education of head: vocational/technical | 0.066* | 0.037 | −0.109* | 0.011 | −0.098* | 0.008 |
| Education of head: university | 0.117* | 0.029 | 0.135* | 0.014 | 0.207* | 0.011 |
| Age of head | 0.021* | 0.005 | 0.017* | 0.002 | 0.011* | 0.001 |
| Age of head squared | −0.000* | 0.000 | −0.000* | 0.000 | −0.000* | 0.000 |
| Female head | −0.117* | 0.025 | −0.063* | 0.009 | −0.058* | 0.007 |
| Household owns enterprise | 0.321* | 0.043 | 0.163* | 0.015 | 0.229* | 0.014 |
| Household owns land | 0.178* | 0.022 | — | — | 0.033* | 0.007 |
| Household is renter | −0.326* | 0.038 | −0.173* | 0.010 | −0.047* | 0.007 |
| Share of wages in household income | 0.318* | 0.036 | 0.172* | 0.018 | 0.141* | 0.012 |
| Number of unemployed in household | — | — | −0.102* | 0.009 | −0.120* | 0.007 |
| Head is unemployed | — | — | — | — | — | — |
| Head is inactive | — | — | −0.035* | 0.017 | −0.007 | 0.011 |
| Location: non-capital city | −0.140* | 0.027 | 0.017 | 0.010 | −0.095* | 0.011 |
| Location: village | −0.246* | 0.033 | −0.007 | 0.011 | −0.198* | 0.013 |
| Number of observations | 2465 | | 8104 | | 16,050 | |
| R² (adjusted) | 0.288 | | 0.301 | | 0.267 | |
| F-statistic | 63.39* | | 205.56* | | 325.47* | |

*Note*: Asterisk (*) indicates that estimated parameters are significantly different from zero at the 90 percent confidence level.

tries (Bulgaria) show strong location effects, while others (Hungary) show almost none.

In Bulgaria, ownership of a household enterprise, owning one's home, and deriving all household income from wages each implies increases of household welfare in excess of 30 percent. No single variable has such high welfare premium attached to it in Hungary or Poland. In Hungary, the strongest effect comes from primary education (negative 23 percent relative to the reference category of secondary education). Enterprise and home ownership, and a wages-only income each add 16–17 percent to household welfare. In Poland, the strongest welfare determinant is also a home enterprise (23 percent), but wage income and home ownership have smaller effects (14 percent and 5 percent, respectively).

The results clearly indicate the key role played by education in transition economies. In Bulgaria, households where the head did not achieve more than primary education have a welfare level 23.5 percent below that of the reference category (a household where the head has secondary education). This welfare "penalty" for low education is similar in the other two countries. Vocational and technical education is associated with a small welfare gain in Bulgaria, relative to secondary education, but with a welfare loss in Hungary and Poland. The likely explanation is that Bulgaria is not yet as far advanced in its transition as the other two countries, and still has many unconverted state industries where the pre-transition vocational and technical education continues to have a high payoff. The conversion process in the other countries has put a premium on job flexibility, and the more general secondary education and especially university education have proved to lend themselves better to the needed adaptation. This is reflected in the higher coefficients for university education in Hungary and Poland relative to Bulgaria.

These results underscore the crucial importance of general education (especially post-secondary education) for a successful long-term strategy in coping with transition. The huge gaps in the return to education between the primary and higher levels point to the unequalizing effect on the distribution of household welfare that is likely to result from transition. It is not practically possible to "upgrade" people's educations in the short run—particularly since almost two-thirds of heads of households in the East European countries have primary or vocational/technical education levels. These households will progressively fall behind as transition proceeds, unless they can be reschooled or retrained. There is evidence that following transition the distribution of wages has become more unequal in Eastern Europe (Milanovic, 1995), and our results indicate that this effect from education extends to the overall distribution of household welfare as well.

The poverty profiles earlier in this chapter, as well as other analyses of poverty in Eastern Europe (Grootaert, 1995, 1997a) have highlighted the strong correlation between poverty and open unemployment. Unemployment is perhaps the most visible aspect of the social cost of transition, and it has severe distributional implications. The results in Table 2.11 indicate that over and above other household attributes (some of which, such as low education, themselves increase the probability of being unemployed), the presence of an unemployed household member reduces household welfare by 10–12 percent.[15] A significant number of households in Eastern Europe have more than one unemployed member.

As one can expect, household size is negatively related to household welfare (since we defined the latter as household expenditure per equivalent adult). However, what is of interest is the role of household composition, as reflected in the magnitude of the coefficients for each type of household member. Except for Bulgaria, the strongest negative coefficient is found for the number of children. The implication is that households do not succeed in maintaining their welfare levels when the number of children increases—despite the generous social transfers in Eastern Europe and the presence of general entitlement programs such as the family allowances, which are targeted on children. Given the positive correlation between household size and poverty, child-oriented transfer programs may well need to move away from being general entitlements to being more poverty-targeted by paying larger amounts to poor families with children.

The pattern of the coefficients of the other demographic variables is country specific. With respect to age of the head of household, each of the three countries indicates an inverted-U life-cycle pattern with welfare levels rising over most of the adult age range, then falling in the elderly years. The turning points are 49 years of age for Bulgaria, 53 years for Hungary, and 68 years for Poland. This may suggest differential effectiveness of the pension system to maintain welfare levels. We discussed the generosity of the Polish pension system previously, but other factors likely play a role, including private transfers and the ability (and willingness) of retired people to earn secondary incomes.

In each of the three countries, female-headed households have lower welfare than male-headed households who are similar in all other characteristics. The shortfall ranges from 5.8 percent in Poland to 11.7 percent in Bulgaria. There appears to be a coincidence of demographic factors. In Poland, old age clearly matters least in terms of its impact on welfare levels (the age turning point is highest, and the coefficient of "number of elderly" in the household composition variables is lowest), and this is also the case for gender effects. In contrast, Bulgaria has the strongest age and gender effects, two to three times larger than those observed in Poland.

Lastly, we need to point at the country-specific location effects. In Hungary, the large welfare differences across locations are fully explained by the distribution of demographic and economic characteristics of households, and residual location effects are not statistically different from zero. In Bulgaria and Poland, in contrast, large location effects remain. Relative to the capital city, households living in other cities have a 10–14 percent lower welfare level, and those in villages are 20–25 percent lower, even after controlling for all household characteristics included in the model. This suggests that economic and social infrastructure, as well as other supply factors of economic activity, have important locational inequalities. Indeed, it has been a characteristic of much of the transition in Eastern Europe that certain regions, such as those with traditional heavy industry, have suffered the most from transition due to the impossibility to convert such industries to privately owned competitive firms. Similarly, the conversion of state-controlled agriculture to private farms has not happened without loss of income to many farmers (Milanovic, 1995).

## Poverty Equations

As we discussed in Section 2.2, we are concerned about the effect of possible measurement error of household expenditure that could be correlated with some of the explanatory variables in the model (e.g., educated people report household expenditures more accurately; older people have more difficulty with reporting; households with self-employment income try to hide income and expenditure for fear of taxation). This could bias the coefficients of the welfare equation estimated by OLS. There is also a concern about the extent to which a given functional form fits the distribution. For both reasons, we estimated poverty equations with a binary dependent variable (poor/non-poor) using probit techniques. The consistency, or lack thereof, of probit results with the welfare equation results serves as a test for the presence of measurement error or functional-form-fit problems.

The results in Table 2.12 suggest that the binary model provides a good fit. The model correctly classifies 77 percent to 82 percent of households as poor or non-poor, and as was the case with the OLS model, almost all of the included variables have estimated coefficients significantly different from zero at the 90 percent confidence level. Table 2.12 does not report the probit coefficients, but the probability derivatives at the mean of each continuous explanatory variable and for a change from zero to one in the case of dummy variables. The estimation used non-poor as the base category, hence the derivatives pertain to the probability to be poor.

Substantively, the pattern of determinants of poverty is entirely consistent with the pattern of determinants of welfare that was revealed by the welfare regression. All factors that are correlated with an increase/decrease in welfare are correlated with a decrease/increase in the probability to be poor. Hence, qualitatively the poverty regression adds nothing to the findings from the welfare regression. However, there are some quantitative differences in terms of the relative magnitude of the effects. This is to be

**Table 2.12.  Poverty equations (probit): East European countries**

| | Bulgaria | | Hungary | | Poland | |
|---|---|---|---|---|---|---|
| | Probability derivatives | Standard error | Probability derivatives | Standard error | Probability derivatives | Standard error |
| Number of children | 0.039* | 0.013 | 0.056* | 0.006 | 0.062* | 0.003 |
| Number of male adults | 0.052* | 0.015 | 0.012 | 0.008 | 0.013* | 0.004 |
| Number of female adults | 0.018 | 0.015 | −0.006 | 0.008 | 0.004 | 0.005 |
| Number of elderly | 0.055* | 0.020 | 0.020* | 0.010 | 0.015* | 0.007 |
| Education of head: primary | 0.171* | 0.024 | 0.188* | 0.014 | 0.161* | 0.010 |
| Education of head: vocational/technical | −0.056 | 0.037 | 0.077* | 0.016 | 0.076* | 0.009 |
| Education of head: university | −0.085* | 0.029 | −0.091* | 0.015 | −0.094* | 0.010 |
| Age of head | −0.014* | 0.004 | −0.016* | 0.002 | −0.008 | 0.001 |
| Age of head squared | 0.000* | 0.000 | 0.000* | 0.000 | 0.000* | 0.000 |
| Female head | 0.113* | 0.027 | 0.031* | 0.011 | 0.027* | 0.007 |
| Household owns enterprise | −0.169* | 0.028 | −0.078* | 0.014 | −0.102* | 0.008 |
| Household owns land | −0.131* | 0.021 | — | — | −0.029* | 0.008 |
| Household is renter | 0.244* | 0.047 | 0.172* | 0.015 | 0.020* | 0.007 |
| Share of wages in household income | −0.272* | 0.037 | −0.136* | 0.021 | −0.122* | 0.012 |
| Number of unemployed in household | — | — | 0.075* | 0.010 | 0.078* | 0.007 |
| Head is unemployed | — | — | — | — | — | — |
| Head is inactive | — | — | −0.001 | 0.018 | −0.022* | 0.010 |
| Location: non-capital city | 0.029 | 0.029 | −0.037* | 0.012 | 0.018 | 0.014 |
| Location: village | 0.128* | 0.037 | −0.002 | 0.013 | 0.092* | 0.017 |
| Log-likelihood | −1199.3 | | −3418.7 | | −6677.6 | |
| Chi-squared | 503.95 | | 1381.3 | | 2291.7 | |
| Prob > chi-squared | 0.0000 | | 0.0000 | | 0.0000 | |
| Percent correct predictions | 76.6 | | 81.22 | | 81.63 | |

*Note*: Asterisk (*) indicates significance of the underlying coefficient at 90 percent confidence level. Derivatives are taken at the mean values of continuous variables or for discrete change of dummy variables from 0 to 1.

expected, of course, since the poverty regression and the welfare regression use different information. A case in point is the effect of education in Poland. In the welfare regression, university education was associated with a 21 percent welfare premium relative to secondary education, while primary education was associated with a welfare reduction of 20 percent—that is, the two levels of education had symmetrical welfare effects around the reference category. In contrast, primary education increases the probability to be poor by 16 percentage points relative to secondary education, but university education reduces it by only 9 percentage points. In other words, university education is an important determinant of where on the welfare distribution a household will end up, and it has large absolute returns, but it has a lesser role as a determinant of poverty.

There are several similar patterns in the shift of relative roles of variables between the welfare regression and the poverty regression. These shifts have implications for the targeting and design of poverty alleviation interventions. Foremost is the role of household enterprises. In Bulgaria and Poland, ownership of a household enterprise makes the largest or second-largest positive contribution to household welfare—a clear reflection of the post-transition emergence of the small-scale private sector. These enterprises do reduce the probability that the household is poor, but the estimated effects are smaller than several other variables, such as education or the share of wages. The contribution of household enterprises is hence more important in the upper part of the distribution, and one characteristic of the poor in transition economies is that they have not yet successfully gotten involved in the private sector as entrepreneurs.

Important differences between the welfare and poverty regressions also occur in the demographic and location variables. While both models underscore the correlation between number of children and low welfare or poverty, they fail to do so for other categories of household members. In Bulgaria and Poland, for example, additional female adults in the household are associated with lower household welfare, but this does not increase the probability to be poor. In Bulgaria, the coefficient for male adults stands out as much higher than in other countries and could indicate the difficulties in that country for men in their prime earning years to find adequately paid employment.

The results for location also deserve highlighting. The degree to which regional or locational targeting of poverty interventions is desirable and useful is frequently a major issue. The answer is different for each country, but it is important to underline that the answer given by the welfare regression is not the same as that given by the poverty regression. This is simply saying that the geographic distribution of welfare is not the same as the geographic distribution of poverty.[16] Specifically, in Bulgaria and Poland, the probability of being poor does not differ between the capital city and other urban areas (after controlling for all other variables), even though the latter areas have significantly lower welfare levels. In the rural areas of these two countries, however, there is a higher probability to be poor, which is consistent with a negative welfare effect. Hungary is unique in that, *ceteris paribus*, the probability of being poor is *less* outside the capital city.

## Quantile Regressions

Table 2.13 presents the results from quantile regressions estimated at the tenth, twenty-fifth, fiftieth, seventy-fifth, and ninetieth percentiles of the distribution of household expenditure per equivalent adult. For space reasons, only selected coefficients are shown. The general observation is that the estimated coefficients show large variations across the distribution, although the patterns are country-specific. The coefficients of education are generally larger (in absolute value) below the median than above it, highlighting the role of education as a determinant of welfare in that range of the distribution. We remind the reader, however, that the estimated coefficients of quantile regressions are conditional upon the values of the independent variables and are not comparable to OLS coefficients (see the discussion in Section 2.2).

In contrast, the coefficients of the enterprise ownership variable, in each of the three countries, are higher at the upper end of the distribution. This confirms what we concluded earlier when comparing the welfare equation with the poverty probit model, namely, that owner-

Table 2.13.  **Quantile regressions: East European countries**

|  | 10% | 25% | Median | 75% | 90% |
|---|---|---|---|---|---|
| | | | **Bulgaria** | | |
| Education of head: primary | −0.209* | 0.229* | −0.211* | −0.225* | −0.225* |
| Education of head: vocational/technical | 0.121* | 0.062 | 0.062 | 0.004 | 0.041 |
| Education of head: university | 0.223* | 0.107* | 0.101* | 0.079* | 0.134* |
| Female head | −0.117* | −0.130* | −0.097* | −0.082* | −0.038* |
| Enterprise ownership | 0.290* | 0.308* | 0.293* | 0.361* | 0.341* |
| Land ownership | 0.198* | 0.149* | 0.164* | 0.127* | 0.089* |
| Share of wages in household income | 0.399* | 0.378* | 0.315* | 0.249* | 0.145* |
| Number of unemployed in household | — | — | — | — | — |
| | | | **Hungary** | | |
| Education of head: primary | −0.247* | −0.256* | −0.220* | −0.227* | −0.224* |
| Education of head: vocational/technical | −0.108* | −0.123* | −0.118* | −0.115* | −0.135* |
| Education of head: university | 0.155* | 0.160* | 0.150* | 0.110* | 0.117* |
| Female head | −0.054* | −0.075* | −0.082* | −0.087* | −0.084* |
| Enterprise ownership | 0.088* | 0.121* | 0.156* | 0.206* | 0.194* |
| Land ownership | — | — | — | — | — |
| Share of wages in household income | 0.161* | 0.174* | 0.178* | 0.184* | 0.114* |
| Number of unemployed in household | −0.134* | −0.123* | −0.106* | −0.086* | −0.094* |
| | | | **Poland** | | |
| Education of head: primary | −0.215* | −0.208* | −0.204* | −0.178* | −0.168* |
| Education of head: vocational/technical | −0.096* | −0.107* | −0.107* | −0.097* | −0.098* |
| Education of head: university | 0.212* | 0.225* | 0.214* | 0.188* | 0.171* |
| Female head | −0.058* | −0.051* | −0.062* | −0.075* | −0.070* |
| Enterprise ownership | 0.222* | 0.210* | 0.215* | 0.252* | 0.231* |
| Land ownership | 0.047* | 0.039* | 0.031* | 0.029* | 0.035* |
| Share of wages in household income | 0.229* | 0.172* | 0.127* | 0.109* | 0.057* |
| Number of unemployed in household | −0.099* | −0.115* | −0.118* | −0.129* | −0.151* |

*Note*: Asterisk (*) indicates that coefficient is significantly different from zero at the 90 percent confidence level.

ship of a household enterprise is more important as an overall determinant of welfare than as a vehicle to escape from poverty. In Bulgaria and Poland, the share of wages in total household income is a much more important determinant of household welfare below the median than above. Clearly, obtaining a wage job is the most important vehicle to improving welfare when one is at the lower end of the distribution.

The impact of unemployment on household welfare is not the

same across countries. In Hungary, the negative effect of unemployment is strongest below the median, while in Poland it is strongest above the median. As we saw earlier, in each of the three East European countries there is a significant negative welfare gap for female-headed households. The quantile regressions indicate that this gap actually increases with income in Hungary and Poland. This is likely a reflection of the effective poverty targeting of the social safety net in these countries, which has successfully reached poor female-headed households (see Chapter 4). In Bulgaria, the reverse is true, and the welfare gap for female-headed household is three to four times larger in the lowest quartile than at the top of the distribution. Also noteworthy is that in Bulgaria, land ownership still plays a critical role as a welfare determinant and is especially important for the poor. Its returns are comparable to those of education.

## Split-Sample Regressions

The discussion so far has highlighted the role of education as a vehicle to improve household welfare in the long run. As we explained in Section 2.2, we split the sample of households into four subsamples based on the education level of the head of household, in order to analyze the interaction between human capital and other household assets. In Bulgaria, a high education level almost doubles the return to owning a household enterprise, but in Poland entrepreneurs with primary education obtain the highest returns. Given that in Poland the overall return to university education is much higher than in Bulgaria (see Table 2.11), we suspect that the well-educated in Poland prefer to wait for a wage job that would realize that return rather than to engage in an alternative career as an entrepreneur. This is confirmed by the strong negative effect of unemployment for well-educated heads of household, which suggests that they do not have alternative income sources. Less educated heads of household in Poland are less impacted by unemployment because they have set up informal enterprises.

In Hungary, the returns to household enterprises vary relatively little with education level, and the highest returns are achieved by people with secondary educations. Wage jobs, on the other hand, have the highest payoff for people with university education.

**Table 2.14. Split-sample results: East European countries**

| | Primary education | Vocational education | Secondary education | University education |
|---|---|---|---|---|
| | **Bulgaria** | | | |
| Female head | −0.100* | −0.011 | −0.201* | −0.110 |
| Enterprise ownership | 0.218* | 0.012 | 0.347* | 0.400* |
| Land ownership | 0.264* | 0.015 | 0.093* | 0.059 |
| Share of wages in household income | 0.399* | 0.148* | 0.157* | 0.284* |
| Number of unemployed in household | — | — | — | — |
| | **Hungary** | | | |
| Female head | −0.043* | −0.075* | −0.069* | −0.090* |
| Enterprise ownership | 0.124* | 0.170* | 0.190* | 0.140* |
| Land ownership | — | — | — | — |
| Share of wages in household income | 0.174* | 0.072 | 0.199* | 0.317* |
| Number of unemployed in household | −0.110* | −0.101* | −0.121* | −0.082* |
| | **Poland** | | | |
| Female head | −0.076* | −0.041* | −0.055* | −0.065* |
| Enterprise ownership | 0.305* | 0.208* | 0.241* | 0.145* |
| Land ownership | 0.038* | 0.031* | 0.040* | 0.016 |
| Share of wages in household income | 0.141* | 0.080* | 0.186* | 0.102* |
| Number of unemployed in household | −0.087* | −0.142* | −0.144* | −0.177* |

*Note*: Asterisk (*) indicates that coefficient is significantly different from zero at the 90 percent confidence level.

## B. Former Soviet Union

### Welfare Equations

For consistency and also owing to a lack of specifications that performed better, the same specification for the OLS model used for Eastern Europe was used for the FSU. In general, the overall goodness of fit for the FSU countries is much lower than for the Eastern

European countries, as shown by the $R^2$ measures reported in Table 2.15. The $R^2$ for Estonia is the only one close to the lower boundary for the East European countries, while the explanatory power of the equation is quite low for both Russia and the Kyrgyz republic. Most but not all of the determinants of welfare included in the specification had estimated parameters significantly different from zero, but there was no discernible pattern to these differences. For all the FSU countries, the number of children, female-headed household, household ownership of an enterprise, the share of wages in household income, university education of the head, and the location dummy variables were significant in determining expenditures per equivalent adult. These significant factors are in most cases easy to measure and can serve as the basis for policy interventions.

As was the case for Eastern Europe, testing the log-linear specification against the linear form (Davidson and MacKinnon, 1981) demonstrated that the log-linear form was preferred. This means, for example, that the effect of adding an additional child is to decrease household welfare (expenditure per equivalent adult) in a fixed proportion, implying that the absolute costs of adding a child are lower for the poor.

In the FSU, locational factors have the strongest effect on household welfare, followed by the share of wages in household income, whether the household has a household enterprise, and higher education. These general findings are discussed in detail below.

In the FSU, the strongest effects on welfare were related to household location, with the sharpest change in household welfare (increasing it by 50 percent) implied by moving from a rural area to the capital in the Kyrgyz republic. Even moving from an urban area to the capital, Bishkek, would increase household welfare by one-third. The location effects are nearly as strong in Russia (43 percent rural-to-capital, 37 percent urban-to-capital) and not inconsiderable in Estonia (with rural-to-capital shifts increasing welfare by nearly one-third).

The dominant role of location, especially location in the capital city, has been documented in other FSU countries such as Armenia and Ukraine (World Bank 1996a, 1995c). In many ways, this finding demonstrates the slowness of transition and of business-encouraging reforms and private sector development, as well as questions of scale in

**Table 2.15.** Welfare equations (OLS): FSU countries
Dependent variable = ln (household expenditure per equivalent adult)

| | Estonia | | Kyrgyz republic | | Russia | |
|---|---|---|---|---|---|---|
| | Parameter estimate | Standard error | Parameter estimate | Standard error | Parameter estimate | Standard error |
| Intercept | 7.301 | 0.089 | 9.627* | 0.191 | 1.068* | 0.120 |
| Number of children | -0.080* | 0.012 | -0.060* | 0.013 | -0.123* | 0.015 |
| Number of male adults | -0.057* | 0.021 | -0.029 | 0.023 | -0.030 | 0.022 |
| Number of female adults | 0.011 | 0.017 | 0.025 | -0.022 | 0.019 | 0.020 |
| Number of elderly | -0.047 | 0.022 | -0.061 | 0.041 | -0.021 | 0.025 |
| Education of head: primary | -0.076* | 0.023 | 0.045 | 0.060 | -0.084* | 0.036 |
| Education of head: vocational/technical | ... | ... | 0.102* | 0.059 | 0.034 | 0.030 |
| Education of head: university | 0.214* | 0.028 | 0.158* | 0.060 | 0.147* | 0.037 |
| Age of head | -0.003 | 0.004 | 0.017* | 0.009 | 0.010* | 0.004 |
| Age of head squared | 0.000 | 0.000 | -0.000* | 0.000 | -0.000 | 0.000 |
| Female head | -0.103* | 0.028 | -0.191* | 0.056 | -0.141* | 0.032 |
| Household owns enterprise | 0.174* | 0.022 | 0.160* | 0.042 | 0.235* | 0.041 |
| Household owns land | 0.160* | 0.021 | 0.249* | 0.040 | -0.043 | 0.029 |
| Household is renter | -0.122* | 0.019 | 0.064 | 0.070 | 0.024 | 0.026 |
| Share of wages in household income | 0.329* | 0.032 | 0.205* | 0.066 | 0.297* | 0.040 |
| Number of unemployed in household | -0.189* | 0.026 | ... | ... | -0.240* | 0.038 |
| Head is unemployed | ... | ... | -0.148* | 0.071 | ... | ... |
| Head is inactive | -0.119* | 0.026 | -0.056 | 0.061 | -0.149* | 0.037 |
| Location: non-capital city | -0.196* | 0.022 | -0.338* | 0.059 | -0.365* | 0.037 |
| Location: village | -0.311* | 0.028 | -0.504* | 0.059 | -0.428* | 0.043 |
| Number of observations | 2817 | | 1929 | | 5147 | |
| $R^2$ (adjusted) | 0.256 | | 0.103 | | 0.115 | |
| F-statistic | 57.95* | | 13.26* | | 38.08* | |

*Note*: Asterisk (*) indicates that estimated parameters are significantly different from zero at the 90 percent confidence level.

many small FSU countries. Aside from Russia (and possibly Ukraine), most FSU countries are quite small in terms of population and GDP, so most private sector development has been concentrated in the capital cities (which are often the only cities of any appreciable size).

The next most significant factors for increasing household welfare in the FSU were the household's entrepreneurial activity, either through owning an enterprise or farming a private plot of land, and the household's link to the labor market, as proxied by the share of wages in total household income. However, the ranking of these factors was country-specific. In Estonia, land ownership and owning an enterprise was significant, but most important was the share of wages in household income, which can increase welfare by one-third. In Russia, land ownership was not significant,[17] but the share of wages in household income and ownership of household businesses were important, raising household welfare 30 and 24 percent respectively. In the Kyrgyz republic, after location, ownership of a private plot had the largest effect on welfare, increasing it by 25 percent, while household welfare increased 20 percent from increasing participation in the official economy (as captured by an increase in the share of wages in total household income).

In all three countries, the presence of an unemployed household head (or household member) was found to significantly decrease household welfare. In Estonia and Russia, specifications based on the number of unemployed demonstrated that adding an unemployed household member reduced household welfare per equivalent adult between 15 and 20 percent, respectively. In the Kyrgyz republic, the dummy variable for household head performed better (partly because of the lower number of "unemployed" in the Kyrgyz republic, where many family members work on the same private plot and are thus automatically not counted as unemployed) and resulted in reductions of welfare in the order of those in Russia. Additionally, in Russia and in Estonia, households headed by individuals not in the labor force (inactive heads) were associated with declines in household welfare of 15 and 12 percent, respectively.

The final significant factor was whether the household head had a university education. In all three countries, welfare gains were approximately 15–20 percent. In Estonia and Russia, primary education of the head was also significant and in the expected (negative) direction, reducing household welfare about 8 percent in both cases. In the Kyrgyz republic, vocational-technical training was also associated with improved welfare—having a household head with it would raise household welfare 10 percent relative to a household head with secondary education. In Russia, however, vocational-technical did not have a significantly different return from secondary education.[18]

Demographic factors, except for the number of children and female headship, were generally not very important for household welfare in the three FSU countries. In each case, adding children meant reducing household welfare, from a low of a 6 percent reduction in the Kyrgyz republic to a 12 percent reduction in Russia. In Russia, there was a system of generalized child allowances, but there were significant payment arrears, and the take-up rate was low. Of families with children under 18, only 60 percent reported receipt of a child allowance (World Bank, 1995b). In the Kyrgyz republic, budgetary sequestration resulted in a withdrawal of the child allowance in 1994, and the substitution of a new benefit, the common monthly subsidy. In Estonia, fiscal austerity resulted in flat-rate pensions in 1993 and a withdrawal of social assistance benefits inherited from the Soviet Union.

In Russia and the Kyrgyz republic, increases in the age of the household head were associated with small increases in household welfare, but only in the Kyrgyz republic was there a discernible U-shaped life-cycle pattern. Other demographic variables were not significant, except for the number of adult males in Estonia.

Overall, these results underscore the critical role of the labor market in determining household welfare in the FSU. Those households that have most effectively captured the returns from their own labor and effort in own family businesses or private plots have been able to stay out of poverty. Individuals with university educations seem to have been best suited to capture the new possibilities as domestic markets have opened up and economic control and regulation relaxed.

The importance of location, household participation in the labor market, and education for household welfare presents formidable challenges to country authorities seeking to reduce poverty and to keep poor households from becoming poorer. Whether a household has a private plot or university-educated head are not easy factors to change in the short run, while the extreme locational disparities are so large as to be unlikely to be rectified in even the longer term. However, the importance of entrepreneurial activity for increasing household welfare may very well be fostered by steps in the short and medium terms, perhaps including public works and micro credit programs. In Russia, where non-governmental organizations have been especially active (Nizhnyy Novgorod, Yekaterinburg), credit unions and small business incubators have been set up.

## Poverty Equations

Given the difficulties of conducting household surveys in the FSU (high refusal rates, extreme reluctance to reveal sensitive information on income and alcohol consumption), it is not surprising that measurement error is a significant concern for the data sets on Estonia, Russia, and the Kyrgyz republic. Additionally, the lower levels of goodness of fit for these FSU countries suggest that a binary dependent variable (poor/non-poor) estimated by probit techniques might perform better and would provide valuable information about some of the variables included. In this sense, lack of consistency between the probit and OLS results would demonstrate problems either with measurement error or in specification.

The probit results in Table 2.16 suggest an acceptable fit, but not a particularly good one. The model serves to predict correctly the poverty status of about three-quarters of Estonian households, but only 60–65 percent of Russian and Kyrgyz republic households. As was the case with the OLS results, not all coefficients were found to be significantly different from zero at a 90 percent confidence level, and a small subset of the coefficients that were significant in the OLS were not significant in the probit (Estonia: primary education and inactive head; Russia: primary education; and the Kyrgyz republic: two education variables and unemployed head). In Russia, the tenancy status of the household was significant in the probit but not in the OLS model.

# Table 2.16. Poverty equations (probit): FSU countries

| | Estonia | | Kyrgyz republic | | Russia | |
|---|---|---|---|---|---|---|
| | Probability derivatives | Standard error | Probability derivatives | Standard error | Probability derivatives | Standard error |
| Number of children | 0.056* | 0.012 | 0.020* | 0.008 | 0.065* | 0.010 |
| Number of male adults | 0.050* | 0.021 | 0.008 | 0.014 | 0.011 | 0.014 |
| Number of female adults | 0.013 | 0.018 | −0.010 | 0.014 | −0.006 | 0.013 |
| Number of elderly | 0.037 | 0.022 | 0.003 | 0.026 | −0.005 | 0.016 |
| Education of head: primary | 0.045 | 0.023 | 0.001 | 0.037 | 0.032 | 0.023 |
| Education of head: vocational/technical | ... | ... | −0.027 | 0.036 | −0.028 | 0.019 |
| Education of head: university | −0.149* | 0.029 | −0.059 | 0.036 | −0.094* | 0.023 |
| Age of head | 0.003 | 0.003 | −0.010* | 0.005 | −0.006* | 0.003 |
| Age of head squared | −0.000 | 0.000 | 0.000* | 0.000 | 0.000 | 0.000 |
| Female head | 0.077* | 0.028 | 0.119* | 0.036 | 0.066* | 0.020 |
| Household owns enterprise | −0.135* | 0.022 | −0.094* | 0.025 | −0.127* | 0.023 |
| Household owns land | −0.159* | 0.022 | −0.092* | 0.025 | 0.010 | 0.018 |
| Household is renter | 0.088* | 0.019 | −0.032 | 0.043 | −0.046* | 0.016 |
| Share of wages in household income | −0.277* | 0.033 | −0.104* | 0.041 | −0.184* | 0.025 |
| Number of unemployed in household | 0.115* | 0.025 | ... | ... | 0.137* | 0.024 |
| Head is unemployed | ... | ... | 0.036 | 0.044 | ... | ... |
| Head is inactive | 0.046 | 0.030 | 0.014 | 0.039 | 0.074* | 0.024 |
| Location: non-capital city | 0.154* | 0.024 | 0.195* | 0.039 | 0.187* | 0.025 |
| Location: village | 0.273* | 0.032 | 0.266* | 0.035 | 0.222* | 0.030 |
| | | | | | | |
| Log-likelihood | −1504.8 | | −1241.5 | | −3201.8 | |
| Chi-squared | 494.53* | | 136.75* | | 478.38 | |
| Prob > chi-squared | 0.000 | | 0.000 | | 0.000 | |
| % correct predictions | 72.6 | | 61.5 | | 65.0 | |

*Note*: Asterisk (*) indicates significance of the underlying coefficient at 90 percent confidence level. Derivatives are taken at the mean values of continuous variables or for discrete change of dummy variables from 0 to 1.

Results of the probit are reported in Table 2.16 as the probability derivatives at the mean levels of continuous variables, and for a discrete 0 to 1 change for the dummy variables. The estimation used non-poor as the base category, so derivatives with a positive sign indicate an increased probability of being poor, and derivatives with a negative sign pertain to reducing the chance of being poor. Other than the four cases reported above where a variable was significant in OLS but not in the probit (or vice versa), the results suggest that the determinants of poverty identified in the probit are essentially the same as the determinants of household welfare discussed in the preceding section.

There are discrete quantitative differences in the coefficients estimated by the two procedures, which is as expected, since the probit equation is based on information different from that of the levels regression, although the rank ordering is much the same (except in the Kyrgyz republic). For example, in Estonia, share of wages in household income (increase of 33 percent) and location in a village (decline of 31 percent) had the largest effects on household welfare. In the probit, these two variables had the largest effect on the probability of the household's being poor, with changes in probability of 28 percent for both, with the appropriate signs. The main exception to the consistency of the findings was for primary education of the household head, which was found to reduce household welfare by 7 percent in the welfare regression but was not significant in the probit regression. Access to land was in fifth place for determining poverty but in eighth place for welfare. Aside from this minor reordering, there were no other significant changes. The first four variables that were most significant for poverty were also the most significant for household welfare: share of wages in household income, location in a village, university education of head, and non-capital city location.

In Russia, two factors (renting one's home and age of head) were associated with poverty in the probit regressions but were not identified as contributing significantly to household welfare, while one factor that did reduce household welfare (primary education for household head) was not significant for poverty. However, these three variables were all relatively unimportant: renting reduced the risk of poverty less than 5 percentage points and age of head by less than one percentage point (the two lowest of the significant variables for poverty), while primary education reduced welfare by about 8 percentage points (the lowest of all significant variables for welfare). More significantly, the ranking of the first five variables remained the same for both poverty and welfare: rural, non-capital city, share of wages in household income, number of unemployed in household, and enterprise ownership.

In the Kyrgyz republic, the picture is less clear. The locational factors that were most significant for household welfare were also for poverty (rural and non-capital city, respectively), but the probit found that female headship was in third place (increasing the risk of poverty by 12 percentage points, while in the OLS, it was in fifth place (reducing welfare by 19 percent). The correspondence unraveled further for other factors. In the OLS, land access was third most important, raising household welfare by nearly 25 percent, but in the probit, land access was in sixth place and reduced the chance of poverty only by approximately 9 percentage points. The education variables that were found to be significant for Kyrgyz household welfare were insignificant in the poverty regressions, and the probit also did not identify an unemployed head as a risk factor for poverty, although it was found to reduce household welfare by nearly 15 percent.

Aside from some of the rerankings in the Kyrgyz republic, the overall pattern of poverty determinants is consistent with the pattern demonstrated by the welfare regressions. The findings represent a challenge for social assistance authorities in the FSU countries, since the factors most significant for household welfare and poverty are extremely difficult to change in the short run: location and share of wages in household income. Demographic characteristics (number of children, female-headed households) were generally statistically significant, but increased the risk of poverty only slightly (usually less than 10 percentage points).

## Quantile Regressions

The results of the quantile regressions for the FSU countries are shown in Table 2.17. There is no very clear pattern in the coefficients of the education variables, mainly because most of them are not significant. Only the returns to university education show a clear rela-

**Table 2.17.  Quantile regressions: FSU countries**

|  | 10% | 25% | Median | 75% | 90% |
|---|---|---|---|---|---|
| | | | **Estonia** | | |
| Education of head: primary | −0.066 | −0.062* | −0.082* | −0.081* | −0.057 |
| Education of head: vocational/technical | — | — | — | — | — |
| Education of head: university | 0.197* | 0.191* | 0.249* | 0.192* | 0.182* |
| Female head | −0.058 | −0.128* | −0.109* | −0.101* | −0.140* |
| Enterprise ownership | 0.132* | 0.190* | 0.173* | 0.238* | 0.211* |
| Land ownership | 0.177* | 0.207* | 0.172* | 0.135* | 0.122* |
| Share of wages in household income | 0.361* | 0.372* | 0.364* | 0.343* | 0.287* |
| Number of unemployed in household | −0.256* | −0.208* | −0.177* | −0.140* | −0.107* |
| | | | **Kyrgyz republic** | | |
| Education of head: primary | 0.197 | 0.057 | 0.061 | 0.062 | 0.044 |
| Education of head: vocational/technical | 0.228* | 0.034 | 0.084 | 0.151* | 0.031 |
| Education of head: university | 0.344* | 0.207* | 0.173* | 0.134* | 0.073 |
| Female head | −0.274* | −0.207* | −0.153* | −0.233* | −0.207* |
| Enterprise ownership | 0.280* | 0.220* | 0.206* | 0.163* | 0.101 |
| Land ownership | 0.390* | 0.312* | 0.197* | 0.121* | 0.188* |
| Share of wages in household income | 0.531* | 0.277* | 0.137* | 0.166* | 0.110 |
| Unemployed head of household | −0.267* | −0.246* | −0.119* | 0.044 | −0.069 |
| | | | **Russia** | | |
| Education of head: primary | −0.183* | −0.050 | −0.038 | −0.064 | −0.057 |
| Education of head: vocational/technical | 0.060 | 0.098* | 0.048 | −0.002 | −0.043 |
| Education of head: university | 0.167* | 0.210* | 0.141* | 0.074* | 0.022 |
| Female head | −0.176* | −0.223* | −0.129* | −0.091* | −0.101* |
| Enterprise ownership | 0.285* | 0.284* | 0.236* | 0.174* | 0.140* |
| Land ownership | −0.082 | −0.075 | −0.004 | −0.001 | −0.044 |
| Share of wages in household income | 0.322* | 0.421* | 0.335* | 0.309* | 0.187* |
| Number of unemployed in household | −0.351* | −0.253* | −0.183* | −0.210* | −0.202* |

*Note*: Asterisk (*) indicates that coefficient is significantly different from zero at the 90 percent confidence level.

tion with the household's position on the welfare distribution. In Russia and the Kyrgyz republic, returns to university education fall dramatically as one moves up the distribution, to the point of becoming insignificant at the ninetieth percentile. This clearly indicates that factors other than education explain high incomes in these countries (including factors not captured in the model). In Estonia, the relative weight of education as an explanatory variable is largely invariant with income (except for a small peak around the median).

The role played by household enterprises in explaining household welfare levels is similar to that of education. In Russia and the Kyrgyz republic, these enterprises are much more important below the median than above, while in Estonia they are most important in the upper quartile of the distribution. A feature that clearly distinguishes the FSU countries from the East European countries is the role of land as an asset. In the FSU, land is generally as important or more important than other assets in explaining household welfare, especially in the Kyrgyz republic and Estonia. This is probably also the case in Russia, but the Russian land data have significant measurement problems (see footnote 17). In each of the three countries the returns to land are higher below the median than above the median. These findings underline the importance of developing a rural development and poverty reduction strategy, perhaps centered on land privatization, which has moved very slowly in most of the FSU. Preliminary findings for Armenia strongly suggested the importance of the 1992 land privatization program in preventing rural poverty (World Bank, 1996a), which was significantly lower than urban poverty in Armenia during 1994.[19]

The welfare regression in Table 2.15 had identified the share of wages as the second most important variable (after location) in determining household welfare, and the quantile regression results show that this matters the most for households at or below the median. Creating wage jobs and improving access to them for less well-off households must remain therefore a cornerstone in labor market policies and poverty alleviation efforts in the FSU. The coefficients of the unemployment variable further underline this, as, in all three countries, the negative effect of unemployment is much higher at the bottom than at the top of the distribution.

Lastly, the pattern of the gender gap in household welfare is not the same in the three countries. In Estonia, there is no gap between male-headed and female-headed households at the tenth percentile, but a large one elsewhere, especially at the ninetieth percentile. In the Kyrgyz republic, the gap is highest at the tenth percentile, and in Russia it is highest throughout the bottom quartile. In the latter two

**Table 2.18.　Split-sample results: FSU countries**

|  | Primary education | Vocational education | Secondary education | University education |
|---|---|---|---|---|
| | | Estonia | | |
| Female head | −0.045 | — | −0.080* | −0.157* |
| Enterprise ownership | 0.233* | — | 0.178* | 0.017 |
| Land ownership | 0.241* | — | 0.136* | 0.157* |
| Share of wages in household income | 0.274* | — | 0.377* | 0.270* |
| Number of unemployed in household | −0.248* | — | −0.130* | −0.267* |
| | | Krygyz republic | | |
| Female head | −0.264* | −0.354* | −0.153 | −0.144 |
| Enterprise ownership | 0.196* | 0.218* | 0.036 | 0.136* |
| Land ownership | 0.189* | 0.190* | 0.326* | 0.335* |
| Share of wages in household income | 0.315* | 0.069 | 0.104 | 0.249* |
| Unemployed head of household | −0.205 | −0.133 | −0.216 | 0.056 |
| | | Russia | | |
| Female head | −0.074 | −0.149* | −0.050 | −0.255* |
| Enterprise ownership | 0.166 | 0.243* | 0.318* | 0.146* |
| Land ownership | −0.173* | −0.027 | 0.016 | 0.096 |
| Share of wages in household income | 0.373* | 0.218* | 0.308* | 0.222* |
| Number of unemployed in household | −0.231* | −0.208* | −0.422* | −0.110 |

*Note*: Asterisk (*) indicates that coefficient is significantly different from zero at the 90 percent confidence level.

countries, the safety net has not been as effective in reaching poor female-headed households as in Estonia.

## Split-Sample Regressions

The results from the welfare regressions over subsamples split by the level of education of the head of household show that education interacts significantly with other household assets (Table 2.18).

The returns to household enterprises are generally higher for people with lower levels of education, although the specific level with the most positive interaction differs across the countries: in Estonia, it is primary education, in the Kyrgyz republic it is vocational education, and in Russia it is secondary education. The returns to land ownership also vary greatly with education. In Estonia and Russia, the returns to land are highest for the people with the least education, but in the Kyrgyz republic, the returns to land are highest for people with secondary or university education.

The results confirm the role of wage jobs for the poor. The gain in household welfare from access to a wage job is highest for household heads with primary education in Russia and the Kyrgyz republic. In Estonia, it is highest for household heads with secondary education. Along the same lines, the effect of unemployment on household welfare is very different at different educational levels, but the pattern is country-specific. The huge negative effect (42 percent) in Russia for people with secondary education stands out.

## 2.5. MEANS TESTING AND INDICATOR-BASED TARGETING

In the previous section we explored the determinants of welfare and poverty. This has provided a number of findings, especially regarding the role of household assets and the link to the labor market, that can be used in the design of poverty reduction programs—either for the targeting of transfers, or in active employment creation policies. In this section, we try to answer the question whether indicator targeting is a feasible modus operandi in such policies. The indicators considered are the economic and demographic household characteristics that we used as regressors in the models. Indicator targeting is useful in situations where an overall means test would be difficult to administer because it is costly or unreliable.

Indicator-based targeting is commonly used in East European and FSU countries for certain components of the social safety net.[20] Family allowances are allocated on the basis of the number of children. Eligibility for social assistance often relies on a combination of indicators pertaining to household size, ownership of durable goods (e.g., car or house), and employment status. It is generally not known how efficient such targeting mechanisms are in correctly identifying the poor.

This can be checked empirically using the welfare or poverty equations we estimated in the previous section, by comparing predicted with actual values of the dependent variable and calculating the percentage of correct predictions. Below we report the results of one such exercise, based on an expanded welfare regression. As we discussed in Section 2.2, the expansion consists of adding variables for "official" income (wages and social transfers) and for ownership of household durables. Due to the endogeneity of these variables, no causal interpretation should be given to the coefficients. The purpose is simply to test their predictive ability. The model was estimated with forward stepwise regression.

The set of regressors—household durables, official income, demographic household characteristics, location, employment status—are all fairly easily identifiable indicators, of the sort that social workers could observe or ask about in the course of a visit to a household to determine eligibility for a transfer program. How well do they identify the poor?

## A.   Eastern Europe

Table 2.19 shows, for the three East European countries, the five and ten best predictors and the results in terms of identifying correctly poor and non-poor households. Overall, the results are impressive: the set of 25–30 indicators included in the model correctly predicts poverty status in about 80 percent of the cases. However, the model is clearly much better in identifying the non-poor, with an accuracy of 90 percent for Bulgaria and 97 percent in the cases of Hungary and Poland. For the poor, the results are much worse, with no model reaching even 50 percent accuracy. Clearly, this is inadequate for real-life application.

The results also show a remarkable robustness to the numbers of indicators used. In the case of Poland, the five best predictors do almost as good a job at identifying poverty status as the full set. In

**Table 2.19.  Stepwise targeting regressions (all observations) East European countries**

|  | Bulgaria | Hungary | Poland |
|---|---|---|---|
|  | Best five predictors | | |
|  | Color TV | Car | Washing machine |
|  | Education: primary | Wage income | Number of children |
|  | Refrigerator | Color TV | Wage income |
|  | Car | Number of children | Car |
|  | Wage income | Education: primary | Number of male adults |
|  | % Correct predictions | | |
| Poor | 47.3 | 13.1 | 16.7 |
| Non-poor | 86.8 | 98.7 | 97.5 |
| All | 75.9 | 81.1 | 82.1 |
|  | Second-best five predictors | | |
|  | Number of children | Renter | Social transfers |
|  | VCR | Number of unemployed | Household enterprise |
|  | Renter | Washing machine | Education: university |
|  | Household enterprise | Education: university | Number of unemployed |
|  | Number of male adults | Household enterprise | Number of female adults |
|  | % Correct predictions | | |
| Poor | 35.5 | 24.7 | 22.7 |
| Non-poor | 92.3 | 97.2 | 96.7 |
| All | 76.6 | 82.4 | 82.6 |
|  | All variables—% Correct predictions | | |
| Poor | 45.4 | 30.7 | 24.8 |
| Non-poor | 90.8 | 96.6 | 97.0 |
| All | 78.3 | 83.1 | 83.2 |

*Note*: Dependent variable is the log of per equivalent adult expenditure. The regressors are the same as in the welfare and poverty regressions with the addition of wage and transfer income and consumer durables.

the case of Hungary, the best five variables identify the non-poor almost perfectly (98.7 percent), but correct identification of the poor improves significantly, from 13 percent to 31 percent, as more indicators are added.

It is noteworthy that several household durables keep coming back across countries as good predictors—car, color TV, and washing machine top the list. These durables clearly identify the rich. Other critical predictors are number of children, ownership of a household enterprise, level of wage income, renting one's home, education, and number of unemployed in the household.

Given the apparent success of the model in identifying the rich, we undertook a second simulation. Suppose that the variable list identified in Table 2.19 was used to correctly identify the upper half of the distribution; how well would the set of indicators do to distinguish poor from non-poor households within the group of households below median welfare level?

The results in Table 2.20 show that the indicators are now quite able to correctly identify poor households: success rates range from a low of 60 percent in Poland to a high of 87 percent in Bulgaria (actual poverty rates in the below-median sample are, respectively, 38 percent and 55 percent). This is a very respectable performance and suggests that such approach is worth considering for real-life application. Moreover, in Hungary and Bulgaria, the same level of correct identification of poor households was achieved with the five best predictors alone.[21] In Poland, going from five predictors to the full set yields an improvement from 54 percent to 60 percent correct predictions for poor households.

Interestingly, the set of predictors that emerges as the best is not very different from those that came out of the estimation over the full sample. Among durables, car and color TV are still the best identifiers. Among the other variables, household composition and official income are now more to the fore.

In summary, this exercise illustrates that a fairly simple set of observable indicators at the household level can be used to correctly identify 90 percent or better of non-poor households. This could serve as a first-step screen to eliminate better-off households from consideration in poverty-oriented programs. In a second step, the

**Table 2.20.  Stepwise targeting regressions (observations below median) East European countries**

|  | Bulgaria | Hungary | Poland |
|---|---|---|---|
|  | | Best five predictors | |
|  | Refrigerator | Color TV | Washing machine |
|  | Color TV | Renter | Number of children |
|  | Education: primary | Car | Wage income |
|  | Land ownership | Number of children | Social transfer income |
|  | Wage income | Wage income | Number of male adults |
|  | | % Correct predictions | |
| Poor | 87.8 | 69.1 | 53.7 |
| Non-poor | 27.3 | 62.0 | 76.1 |
| All | 60.6 | 64.8 | 67.6 |
|  | | Second-best five predictors | |
|  | Number of male adults | Refrigerator | Car |
|  | Number of children | Number of unemployed | Color TV |
|  | Age of head of household | Education: primary | Number of unemployed |
|  | Car | Social transfer income | Number of elderly |
|  | Social transfer income | Sewing machine | Number of female adults |
|  | | % Correct predictions | |
| Poor | 87.3 | 65.6 | 57.8 |
| Non-poor | 32.5 | 70.9 | 74.8 |
| All | 62.7 | 68.8 | 68.3 |
|  | | All variables—% Correct predictions | |
| Poor | 86.7 | 67.8 | 60.4 |
| Non-poor | 35.9 | 70.9 | 75.0 |
| All | 63.9 | 69.7 | 69.5 |

*Note*: Dependent variable is the log of per equivalent adult expenditure. The regressors are the same as in the welfare and poverty regressions with the addition of wage and transfer income and consumer durables.

same indicators can be used to identify the poor from the non-poor in the remaining bottom part of the distribution. Success rates in this exercise were in the 60–87 percent range, which is far better than what current social assistance systems in Eastern Europe achieve. Grootaert (1995, 1997a) has documented leakage rates of 47 percent of households in Poland and almost 90 percent in Hungary in the case of social assistance.

There is thus significant scope to improve the targeting of social assistance and other poverty-oriented programs, and the simulation reported here indicates that indicator-based targeting can make a significant contribution. Our results suggest also that the list of indicators will need to be country-specific. While our results are indicative of the potential of indicator-based targeting, they are not a blueprint for practical application. Specifically, results could undoubtedly be improved by testing alternative combinations of variables and by modifying scoring procedures. For example, the best predictors can be given a greater weight than what the regression implicitly gives them. This would improve results, and our findings must therefore be seen as a low-end estimate of the effectiveness of indicator-based targeting to identify poor households.

## B. Former Soviet Union

The regression findings for FSU clearly suggested a link between welfare and poverty and such easily identified household attributes as location, the number of children and elderly members, and whether the household is female-headed. Certain traits, such as the link to the formal labor market and a household enterprise, were associated with higher levels of welfare.

Under the previous Soviet social welfare system, all benefits were categorical ones (see Chapter 3). For example, all males age 60 and over received some sort of pension (regardless of whether they continued to work), which was also the case for all females age 55 and above. Starting in 1992, all children under the age of 16 (or 18 if they were full-time students) were eligible for a general child allowance. Certain categories of people, particularly the disabled, received diverse benefits, such as free or reduced-price utilities and transportation services.

Since most of those who received such categorical benefits were demonstrated to actually be the non-poor (see various World Bank poverty assessments), categorical targeting received significant and warranted criticism from external and internal advisors and policy-makers. However, the problem with categorical targeting may have been in the poor *choice* of categories rather than in the principle of using categories to identify the poor. The choice of categories was dictated by political considerations, not by a careful study of who was poor and what determined poverty.

In this section, we try to determine whether a combination of indicators can identify the poor, which in turn would provide the necessary information for effective targeting of cash or in-kind benefits, or for active labor market policies. The indicators used here are the same economic and demographic variables that were regressors in our previous models, with some additional variables. In practice, in the FSU and particularly in Russia and Ukraine, benefits are being awarded increasingly to applicants who meet a categorical filter *and* an income test. Typically, this means test is based only on official income. As noted in the poverty profile section, in the FSU official income is a particularly poor predictor of household welfare because of the pervasive informal sector and the general unwillingness of households to disclose such sensitive information.

Preliminary evidence from the housing allowance subsidy programs in Ukraine and Russia, which are based on official income (wages plus transfer income), suggests that an official income test has a very high error of exclusion (those who are actually poor are not receiving the benefit). Partly this originates from the very different goal of these programs, which is to promote housing privatization, and partly it may originate from a lack of consideration of other factors related to poverty that are not captured in official income.

In order to improve means testing where it currently exists, and to revise and update the categorical approach overall, we estimate an expanded welfare equation with variables added for official income (wages and social transfers) and for ownership of household durables. The data in Table 2.21 show that the proxy means test was able to identify correctly the poverty/non-poverty status of approximately 64–75 percent of the population, with all three countries having better predictions for the non-poor than for the poor. Only about 60 percent (57–62) of the poor were identified correctly, but this still represents a significant improvement over the previous single-indicator/categorical approach used to allocate benefits such as old-age pensions and student stipends.[22]

At first glance, the five best predictors for the FSU countries seem to be more related to the non-poor side of the spectrum (wage income, car, color TV, household business, university education, land ownership) than to the poor (transfer income). The addition of the next five (best ten total) predictors shows a mixture of factors associated with higher welfare (stereo, car, household enterprise) as with low welfare (number of children, transfer income, rural location, other urban location, number of unemployed, inactive head). This addition does little to improve the fit, raising the overall correct prediction rate only slightly (64–73 percent) and the rate for the poor a bit more (57–58 percent) than was observed by using only the five best predictors. The full model shows a barely greater prediction accuracy.

Given the presence of so many variables associated with the higher end of the welfare distribution and the higher identification rates for the non-poor, we undertook a second simulation similar to what was done for the East European countries, but we found vastly different results. If there was some way to screen out the upper portion of the distribution, how well would the proxy means test distinguish among the poor and non-poor in the lower half of the distribution? For the East European simulation, we assumed that the screen would correctly identify the upper half of the distribution, since the identification rates for the non-poor were all above 90 percent. Although this was a reasonable assumption for Eastern Europe, in the original expanded regression for the FSU countries, only 70–80 percent of the non-poor were correctly identified, thus making this assumption a bit more questionable. However, for consistency, we simply reran the expanded welfare regression via forward stepwise regression on the half of the FSU samples with welfare below the median.

The results in Table 2.22 demonstrate that such an assumed

screen would somewhat improve the identification of the poor in Estonia (from 62 percent to 66 percent correctly identified) but would improve the identification of the poor much more in Russia and the Kyrgyz republic, increasing to 80 and 83 percent, respectively. Of course, there is a cost to this—the few non-poor that remained in the below-median sample were either badly identified (Estonia), very badly identified (Russia), or virtually unidentified (Kyrgyz republic). This suggests that a proxy means test system could perform rather well in Russia and the Kyrgyz republic, and acceptably well in Estonia, provided that an effective mechanism could be found to screen out the upper portion of the welfare distribution. In all three cases even without the screen, the proxy means test would represent a significant improvement over the old categorical approach.

Further, in all three countries, the five best predictors alone did as good a job in identifying the poor (Kyrgyz republic, Russia) or almost as well (Estonia) as did the full model, implying that only a few key data would be required for collection. As in Eastern Europe, the set of predictors that emerges as the best for identifying the poor (given that the upper 50 percent of the distribution was screened out of consideration) is more or less the same as the set that resulted from estimation over the full sample. Interestingly enough, for the Kyrgyz republic, using the below-median observations resulted in only six variables meeting the entry criteria for the forward stepwise regression: land ownership, wage income, car, motorcycle, renter status, and washing machine. For Russia and Estonia, more than ten variables entered into the forward stepwise specification.[23]

Overall, the acceptability of the proxy means test for the FSU countries depends on the reasonability of the assumed screening device. Unlike in Eastern Europe, 90 percent or more of the non-poor cannot be assumed to be removed from consideration through an inventory of their consumer durables and other factors. Only about 70–80 percent of the non-poor could be removed at best in the FSU. Once the non-poor are removed from consideration, virtually the same information collected could be used to further refine the identification of the poor and non-poor in the remaining portion of the welfare distribution, resulting in identification rates of 65–82 percent. Although the potential of proxy means testing in FSU is not quite as impressive as in Eastern Europe, it could still be a significant improvement over the existing system of categorical indicators, which is plagued by very large leakage to the non-poor.

## 2.6. SUMMARY AND CONCLUSIONS

Poverty has emerged as a significant problem in the transition economies. Although more widespread in the former Soviet Union, much "transitional" poverty has proved to be difficult to eradicate even in Eastern Europe. The social protection systems of the transition countries have been inadequate to meet the challenges of transition, being both poorly targeted and costly. Although the open incidence of poverty increased everywhere during the transition period, distinctly different patterns of poverty emerged in Eastern Europe and the former Soviet Union. In general, poverty correlates are more sharply defined in Eastern Europe than in FSU, holding out the potential for better targeting in Eastern Europe.

In this chapter, we undertook a comparative analysis of poverty in three East European countries and three FSU countries. We used the HEIDE data set, specially constructed for that purpose. The analysis consisted of three tasks: a profile of the incidence and depth of poverty using aggregate poverty indexes (Section 2.3); a multivariate analysis of the determinants of poverty (Section 2.4); and an empirical evaluation of the role of means testing and indicator-based targeting in poverty alleviation programs (Section 2.5).

We also raised a number of methodological issues. For the poverty profile, we used the well-known P-alpha class of poverty indexes, disaggregated along relevant socioeconomic and demographic dimensions. We opted, however, for a relative poverty line, rather than the more customary approach of absolute lines in cross-country research. In doing so, we put the comparability of the poverty profile ahead of the comparability of the head count. When countries have significantly different levels of GDP, the same absolute line would cut off from very small to very large proportions of the population, which are difficult to disaggregate and compare in a meaningful way.

For the multivariate analysis we took note of the current debate over welfare regressions and binary poverty regressions as the main analytic tool for poverty research, but we argued that in transition economies both are needed as they serve different purposes. While welfare regresssions utilize the maximum available statistical information on the dependent variable, they ignore measurement errors of the type typically present in transition economy databases. In our results, the two models provided qualitatively consistent answers on the significant determinants of poverty and welfare, but underlined that some variables, such as education and productive assets, play different roles in escape from poverty as opposed to determining position on the non-poor segment of the welfare distribution.

Likewise, the quantile regressions estimated at different points of the household welfare distribution, as well as the results from splitting the sample according to the level of education of the head of household, suggest that the impact of household characteristics on welfare are not the same for the poor and the non-poor. These results call for caution when relying on one single multivariate model to study the correlates of poverty. We would argue that the set of models used here (OLS Welfare Model, Probit Poverty Model, quantile regressions, and split-sample regressions) constitute a useful minimal set to investigate the determinants of poverty.

Using the criterion of two-thirds of household expenditure per equivalent adult (OECD equivalence scale), poverty in Eastern Europe was found to be significantly lower than in FSU countries. Hungary and Poland have the lowest poverty incidence (21–23 percent) and a poverty gap less than 15 percent of the poverty line. Bulgaria is slightly worse off with a poverty rate of 26 percent and a poverty gap of 20 percent. Each of the FSU countries exceeds those statistics by far. Estonia has a poverty incidence of 30 percent and a poverty gap of 20 percent. In Russia and the Kyrgyz republic, the poverty rate is around 40 percent and the poverty gap is in the 25–30 percent range.

The profile of poverty shows some common aspects for Eastern Europe and the former Soviet Union as well as pronounced differences:

- Rural poverty is higher than urban poverty; within urban areas, the capital city has the lowest poverty (except in Hungary); however, in the East European capitals, the poverty gap was higher than elsewhere in the country.
- In Eastern Europe, there is a very strong correlation between poverty incidence and the number of children in the household; in the FSU this is less pronounced, except in Russia.
- Single-person households, especially elderly females, have very high poverty rates (except in Poland); their poverty is also more severe.
- Consistent with this, pensioner households have above-average poverty incidence and gap (except in Poland).
- However, the highest poverty rates are found among people who have lost an active or regular connection with the labor market and live on social transfers (other than pensions) or other non-earned income as prime source of revenue; their poverty rates can be as much as three times higher than the national average, especially if two or more household members are unemployed; these households often absorbed the highest social cost of transition by failing to obtain a regular source of earnings.
- The poverty gap is remarkably uniform in East European countries, especially in Poland and Hungary, indicating that social safety nets have prevented the emergence of deep pockets of poverty. In the FSU, this is much less the case, and frequently those with the highest poverty rate also have the highest poverty gap.
- The key role of labor market connections should not lead to the conclusion that there is no poverty among the working class. Many have little education (primary education or less) or outdated vocational/technical education, and while poverty rates are low for workers, their sheer mass in the total population means that the working poor constitute the largest group of poor.
- The connection between education and poverty suggests that only those with special skills or university education succeed

in escaping poverty in great numbers, thanks to demand for their skills from the newly emerging private sector.

- Last, the profile shows that there is a gender dimension to poverty in each country. Female-headed households have higher poverty incidence and gap in each of the six countries.

Without wishing to downplay differences across countries, the common aspects in this profile of poverty suggests that a case can be made for a poverty alleviation policy for the Eastern Europe/FSU region as a whole. Lessons learned in one country are likely to have applicability in others. Priorities in targeting (children, elderly, low-educated workers, female-headed households) are similar across countries, and the design of targeted interventions can benefit from region-wide experiences. Needless to say, social and cultural differences are important, and must be given their due weight, even if economic behavior and responses are similar.

The multivariate analysis has corroborated the univariate observations from the poverty profile and made it possible to compare net effects, controlling for all other factors, and identify the highest pay-off actions. Although there is more variation across countries, some common factors have emerged:

- Education plays a key role in welfare improvements. There is always a significant welfare penalty to having achieved only primary education, and in some countries (those most advanced in the transition process) the penalty extends to those with vocational and technical educations as well. Since it is not practical to quickly upgrade education or retrain huge segments of the population, this aspect of poverty will remain a long-term challenge.
- Ownership of a household enterprise has very high payoffs in several countries, often increasing household welfare by 20–30 percent. Unquestionably, programs of information, micro-credit, marketing, small-business incubators, and other efforts to help entrepreneurs and prospective entrepreneurs must take center stage in poverty alleviation in Eastern Europe and FSU. There is every reason to believe that in the

short to medium term, employment creation will be much higher in the informal sector than in the formal (often still-to-be-privatized) sector.

- Age and gender effects are of concern in some countries (Bulgaria, Kyrgyz republic) but not in others like Poland, where the pension system has adequate reach. This is primarily an issue of retargeting pensions and other social transfers, or of increasing the level of the minimum pension (paid primarily to women who lack adequate work tenure to receive higher old-age pensions), at the expense of compressing the rest of the pension distribution.

The multivariate analysis has confirmed the importance of household composition, especially the number of children: households do not succeed in maintaining their welfare levels when the number of children increases. This calls for child-oriented transfer programs to move away from general entitlements to means-tested or proxy means-tested programs.

In the final section of this chapter, we undertook an assessment of the potential of proxy means testing and indicator targeting for poverty alleviation programs such as social assistance. We used a set of easily identifiable household characteristics, including demographic composition, education, employment status, location, household durables, and official income to estimate a forward stepwise regression to identify the best predictors. The results for Eastern Europe were more promising than for FSU. In a first run, we could successfully identify more than 90 percent of non-poor households, using a set of 25–30 indicators. A surprising but potentially very important result was that this accuracy was only marginally reduced when the best five or ten predictors were used. In a second run, limited to the lowest half of the distribution (assuming that the first run had successfully identified households in the top half), we correctly identified 60–87 percent of the poor. Again, the loss in accuracy was small when using only the best five or ten predictors. These are very respectable results and suggest that such an approach is worth considering for real-life application.

In the FSU countries, the first-stage correct identification of non-poor households achieved only 69–77 percent, and in the second stage the poor were correctly predicted 65–83 percent of the time. These results are still far better than the systems currently in place in the FSU countries. In Russia, experiments are currently being undertaken with indicator targeting to see how alternative formulas and sets of indicators can improve correct identification of needy social assistance recipients.

**Annex 2.1.   Means and standard deviations of variables
(East European countries)**

|  | Bulgaria | | Hungary | | Poland | |
|---|---|---|---|---|---|---|
|  | Mean | Standard deviation | Mean | Standard deviation | Mean | Standard deviation |
| Household size | 2.92 | 1.56 | 2.78 | 1.33 | 3.13 | 1.61 |
| Number of children | 0.47 | 0.80 | 0.58 | 0.90 | 0.75 | 1.06 |
| Number of male adults | 0.98 | 0.84 | 0.90 | 0.74 | 1.00 | 0.78 |
| Number of female adults | 1.02 | 0.79 | 0.97 | 0.67 | 1.09 | 0.69 |
| Number of elderly | 0.45 | 0.66 | 0.33 | 0.59 | 0.28 | 0.56 |
| Age of head of household | 55.04 | 15.31 | 49.2 | 16.3 | 48.7 | 14.8 |
| Age of head squared | 3264.2 | 1694.4 | 2682.1 | 1703.9 | 2594.3 | 1537.5 |
| Female head of household | 0.21 | 0.41 | 0.31 | 0.46 | 0.35 | 0.48 |
| Head with primary education | 0.47 | 0.50 | 0.43 | 0.49 | 0.33 | 0.47 |
| Head with secondary education | 0.31 | 0.46 | 0.22 | 0.41 | 0.26 | 0.44 |
| Head with vocational/ technical education | 0.07 | 0.26 | 0.24 | 0.43 | 0.32 | 0.46 |
| Head with university education | 0.15 | 0.35 | 0.11 | 0.32 | 0.10 | 0.30 |
| Tenancy status: renter | 0.07 | 0.26 | 0.17 | 0.38 | 0.45 | 0.50 |
| Household enterprise ownership | 0.05 | 0.21 | 0.08 | 0.27 | 0.06 | 0.23 |
| Land ownership | 0.40 | 0.49 | — | — | 0.50 | 0.50 |
| Share of wages in total household income | 0.29 | 0.32 | 0.40 | 0.36 | 0.38 | 0.39 |
| Number of unemployed household members | — | — | 0.21 | 0.49 | 0.16 | 0.42 |
| Unemployed head of household | — | — | 0.05 | 0.22 | 0.02 | 0.15 |
| Inactive head of household | — | — | 0.36 | 0.48 | 0.35 | 0.48 |
| Capital city | 0.15 | 0.36 | 0.22 | 0.41 | 0.07 | 0.26 |
| Other city | 0.52 | 0.50 | 0.41 | 0.49 | 0.60 | 0.49 |
| Rural areas | 0.33 | 0.47 | 0.37 | 0.48 | 0.33 | 0.47 |

## Annex 2.2. Means and standard deviations of variables (FSU countries)

| | Estonia | | Russia | | Kyrgyz republic | |
|---|---|---|---|---|---|---|
| | Mean | Standard deviation | Mean | Standard deviation | Mean | Standard deviation |
| Household size | 2.41 | 1.34 | 2.75 | 1.39 | 4.93 | 2.76 |
| Number of children | 0.51 | 0.85 | 0.59 | 0.86 | 1.82 | 1.70 |
| Number of male adults | 0.70 | 0.68 | 0.82 | 0.72 | 1.39 | 1.07 |
| Number of female adults | 0.88 | 0.65 | 0.98 | 0.68 | 1.48 | 1.01 |
| Number of elderly | 0.32 | 0.58 | 0.35 | 0.60 | 0.24 | 0.50 |
| Age of head of household | 48.10 | 16.41 | 48.40 | 15.75 | 41.16 | 14.00 |
| Age of head squared | 2582.50 | 1656.80 | 2590.70 | 1620.40 | 1889.60 | 1304.50 |
| Female head of household | 0.36 | 0.48 | 0.29 | 0.46 | 0.18 | 0.38 |
| Head with primary education | 0.28 | 0.45 | 0.28 | 0.45 | 0.33 | 0.47 |
| Head with secondary education [1] | 0.58 | 0.49 | 0.34 | 0.47 | 0.24 | 0.43 |
| Head with vocational/ technical education [1] | ... | ... | 0.16 | 0.37 | 0.25 | 0.43 |
| Head with university education | 0.13 | 0.34 | 0.25 | 0.43 | 0.18 | 0.38 |
| Tenancy status: renter | 0.50 | 0.50 | 0.55 | 0.50 | 0.08 | 0.27 |
| Household enterprise ownership | 0.22 | 0.41 | 0.08 | 0.28 | 0.32 | 0.47 |
| Land ownership | 0.53 | 0.50 | 0.23 | 0.42 | 0.58 | 0.49 |
| Share of wages in total household income | 0.45 | 0.39 | 0.43 | 0.39 | 0.27 | 0.33 |
| Number of unemployed household members | 0.11 | 0.37 | 0.08 | 0.30 | ... | ... |
| Unemployed head of household | ... | ... | ... | ... | 0.08 | 0.27 |
| Inactive head of household | 0.32 | 0.47 | 0.34 | 0.47 | 0.22 | 0.42 |
| Capital city | 0.47 | 0.50 | 0.61 | 0.49 | 0.26 | 0.44 |
| Other city | 0.26 | 0.44 | 0.28 | 0.45 | 0.59 | 0.49 |
| Rural areas | 0.27 | 0.44 | 0.10 | 0.31 | 0.17 | 0.37 |

*Note:*
[1] It was not possible to separate household heads with vocational-technical education from heads with general secondary education in Estonia, due to lack of comparability between definitions used in the Estonia survey and those used in other countries.

# CHAPTER 3

# THE ROLE OF SOCIAL ASSISTANCE IN ADDRESSING POVERTY

BRANKO MILANOVIC

## 3.1. WHAT SOCIAL ASSISTANCE DOES: COUNTRY SURVEYS

In this section, we review how social assistance operates and what its effects are in five countries: Poland, Hungary, Bulgaria, Estonia, and Russia. The structure of each country survey is the same. We look first at who is eligible for social assistance and who the actual recipients are (where they are located along the welfare distribution curve); we then look at how much money in total is disbursed for social assistance; how much of total household expenditures are covered by social assistance and how much of the poverty gap is closed; at the end we look at the poor who do not receive social assistance. This uniform structure has both advantages and drawbacks. The advantage is that countries can be easily compared. The disadvantage is that the discussion is necessarily repetitive. However, this was the only way that a very large mass of data for each country could be presented to the reader. The reader is advised to pick and choose what he or she wants to read in this section. If she is interested in learning about the effects of social assistance in one or two countries, she can read only these country reviews. If she is interested simply in a comparison of the performance of different countries, she can almost entirely skip this section and move to the next.

## A.  Poland

*Eligibility for social assistance.* At the time of the Polish survey (1993, all data expressed in June 1993 prices), a household would, in principle, be qualified for social assistance if its monthly per capita income was less than the minimum pension, which in June 1993 amounted to zl. 1,231,000 ($72) per month. The qualifier "in principle" is important because having income below that level was a necessary but not a sufficient condition to receive social assistance. In addition to having low income, a household also needed to fulfill one of 11 "dysfunctionality" conditions, for example to have long-term unemployed members, to be headed by a single parent, to have alcoholism or drug-related problems, protracted illness, and so on.[1] This poverty line was high: it amounted to 77 percent of average monthly per capita expenditures.

*The poor.* A total of 32.4 percent of households had income per capita lower than the poverty threshold, and 37.5 percent of households had expenditures per capita below the threshold level. About a quarter of the households were both expenditure- and income-poor (see Table 3.1).[2] We shall treat the expenditure-poor, the 37.5 percent of households, as "the poor"—that is, as the households that, in principle, should be the object of social assistance. Our decision to use expenditures rather than income is motivated by the fact (discussed in Chapter 2) that expenditures, particularly during the transition, are a more reliable indicator of one's real economic status.

**Table 3.1.   Poland: Who receives social assistance?**

| | Total | Eligible for assistance (expenditure-poor) | Not eligible for assistance (non-poor) |
|---|---|---|---|
| All households | 100 | 37.5 | 62.5 |
| Receiving SA | 3.7 | 2.4 | 1.3 |
| Income-poor | 32.4 | 25.2 | 7.2 |
| Receiving SA | 100 | 64.5 | 35.5 |

| | | Receiving assistance | Not receiving assistance |
|---|---|---|---|
| All poor | 100 | 6.3 | 93.7 |
| Hard-core poor | 100 | 7.5 | 92.5 |
| All non-poor | 100 | 2.1 | 97.9 |

*Note*: Hard-core poor are defined as both income- and expenditure-poor. SA = social assistance.

*Who are the recipients?* Figure 3.1 illustrates where along the income distribution spectrum were the households recipients of social assistance.[3] On the horizontal axis are households ranked according to their per capita expenditures and divided into percentiles from the poorest to the richest. On the vertical axis, we show the percentage of households (within each percentile) who have received social assistance. For example, about 10 percent of households belonging to the several poorest percentiles received social assistance. This value is represented by a dot. The percentile dots are connected by a solid line to show broader trends. The same type of graph is repeated in the rest of the section.[4]

Overall 3.7 percent of households report receiving some social assistance (see the horizontal line drawn at y = 3.7 in Figure 3.1). The vertical line at x = 38 divided the households into the poor and non-poor. Among the poor, the share of social assistance recipients was 6.3 percent; among the non-poor, 2.1 percent. The share of recipients (or differently put, the simple probability of receipt of social assistance) clearly declines with level of welfare (see the solid line in Figure 3.1). Among the poorest, one household in ten receives

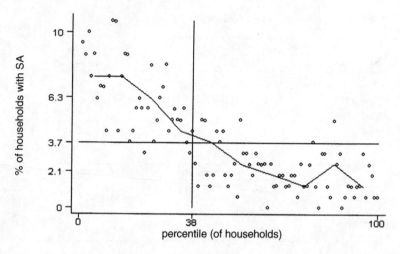

*Note*: Mean calculated across households.

**Figure 3.1. Poland: Percentage of households recipients of social assistance by level of welfare (expenditures per capita)**

some social assistance; among the richest, less than one in one hundred does.

All households who are to the right of the x = 38 line—all those who are non-poor—should not in principle receive social assistance. Everything to the right of that line is therefore leakage. In terms of the number of recipients, 35.5 percent is leakage (see Table 3.1). It is noticeable, though, that for almost all percentiles greater than 38, the percent of households who receive social assistance is below the overall mean of 3.7. In effect, the two lines drawn at y = 3.7 and x = 38 divide the area into four quadrants, two of which are almost empty. Therefore, broadly speaking, probability of a poor household receiving social assistance is always greater than the mean (overall) probability, and probability of a non-poor household receiving assistance is always less than the mean.

The recipients of social assistance are (measured by their household per capita income) a quarter poorer than the average person in Poland (Table 3.2). That difference, however, is very small among

**Table 3.2.   Poland: Social assistance—Reduction of the poverty gap and leakage**

|  | Total | The poor | The non-poor |
|---|---|---|---|
| Social assistance (Zl. billion) | 0.548 | 0.360 | 0.188 |
|  | (100) | (65.7) | (34.3) |
| In billion zloty p.m. |  |  |  |
| Expenditures | 74.212 | 21.936 | 52.276 |
| Expenditure of those with SA > 0 | 2.470 | 1.350 | 1.120 |
| Income | 79.894 | 26.391 | 53.502 |
| Poverty gap | 8.839 | 8.839 | 0 |
| Social assistance as percentage of |  |  |  |
| Expenditures | 0.74 | 1.6 | 0.4 |
| Expenditure of those with SA > 0 | 22.1 | 26.6 | 16.8 |
| Income | 0.74 | 1.4 | 0.35 |
| Poverty gap | 6.2 | 4.1 | — |
| Social assistance per recipient household |  |  |  |
| (Zl. 000/$ p.m.) | 927 ($54) | 945 ($55) | 895 ($52) |
| Expenditure per capita of those *with* |  |  |  |
| social assistance ($ p.m.) a/ | $70 | $50 | $108 |
| *Memo*: Expenditure per capita (overall |  |  |  |
| average $ p.m.) a/ | $93 | $52 | $117 |
| HH size (overall average) | 3.25 | 4.15 | 2.7 |

*Note*: In Warsaw June 1993 prices. Exchange rate: Zl. 17,300 = $1. p.m. = per month. SA = social assistance. HH = household.
a/ Mean across households.

the subset of the poor: poor recipients and poor non-recipients have practically the same expenditures ($50 vs. $52 per capita per month).

*How much do they get?* Figure 3.2 shows the average amounts of social assistance (in '000 zloty per month) received by each per-centile. The average amount of social assistance was zl. 34,100 (see horizontal line in Figure 3.2) or $2 per household per month, with zl. 60,100 ($3.50) among the poor and zl. 18,600 ($1.10) among

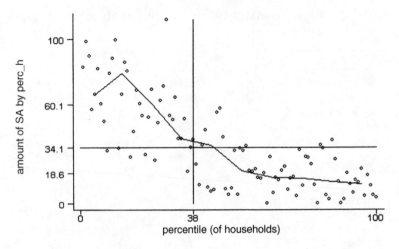

Note: Mean calculated across households.

**Figure 3.2. Poland: Amounts of received social assistance (in '000 Zl. per household per month) by level of welfare (expenditure per capita)**

the non-poor. Since we know that 3.7 percent of households were recipients of social assistance, we can readily calculate that the average amount of assistance given was about $54 per recipient household ($2 divided by 0.037). Among the poor, the average amount was $55, among the non-poor $52 (Table 3.2). The difference between the poor and non-poor in terms of access to social assistance was not in the amounts they received, but in the probability of receiving it. (This fact can also be seen by comparing Figures 3.1 and 3.2 whose shapes are very similar—as they would be if the amounts of social assistance given are the same across the board).

*How much of the poverty gap is closed by social assistance?* The total monthly expenditure-based poverty gap calculated from the *Household Budget Survey* is zl. 8.8 billion as compared to total monthly expenditures of zl. 74.2 billion, or income of zl. 79.9 billion

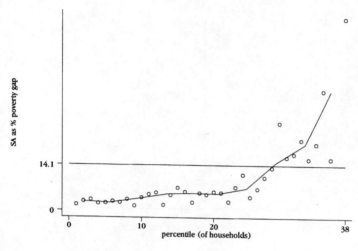

Note: Mean calculated across households.

**Figure 3.3. Poland: Social assistance received as percentage of the poverty gap by level of welfare (expenditure per capita)**

(Table 3.2). Thus, to close the entire poverty gap one would have needed to transfer to the poor and to the poor only almost 12 percent of total population expenditures. But total social assistance (in the sample) amounted to zl. 0.55 billion, that is, 6.2 percent of what is needed to close the entire poverty gap. Moreover, out of zl. 0.55 billion, only zl. 0.36 billion was disbursed to the poor. The well-targeted social assistance was therefore equal to 4.1 percent of the poverty gap,[5] and eliminated 3.9 percent of the (pre-social assistance) poverty gap.[6]

If we look across households as in Figure 3.3 at how much of the poverty gap is eliminated by social assistance rather than at the overall money values, it turns out that the average elimination of the poverty gap is 14.1 percent.[7] The percentage is fairly steady up to the twenty-fifth percentile. Afterwards, it increases fast since the poverty gap declines much faster than the probability of receipt of social assistance.[8] For the thirty-seventh and thirty-eighth percentile social

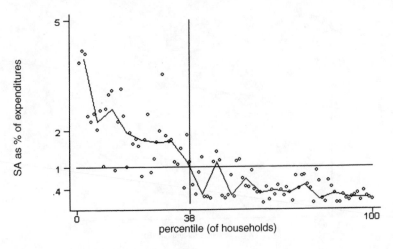

Note: Mean calculated across households.

**Figure 3.4. Poland: Social assistance as percentage of household expenditures by level of welfare**

assistance exceeds, respectively, 100 percent and 50 percent of the poverty gap.

*How much of total expenditures is financed by social assistance?* On average, social assistance accounts for 1 percent of total household expenditures (averaged across households; see Figure 3.4) or 0.74 percent in money terms (see Table 3.2). Among the poor, social assistance pays for 2 percent of expenditures, among the rich for 0.4 percent only. While these percentages are small, among those who did receive social assistance, it covered (on average) 22 percent of expenditures, with 26.6 percent among the poor and 16.8 percent among the non-poor (Table 3.2).

*The poor who do not receive social assistance.* Overall, 93 percent of the poor receive no social assistance. The percentage of the excluded poor declines slightly as one moves toward the more poor (see Figure 3.5), a fact that indicates some improvement in targeting with increasing depth of poverty.

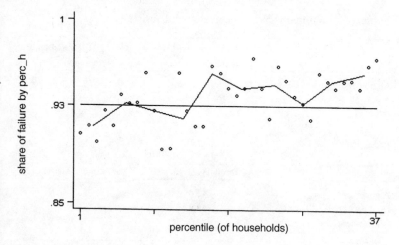

**Figure 3.5. Failure to deliver social assistance (share of poor who do not receive social assistance)**

## B.   Hungary

*Eligibility for social assistance.* At the time of the Hungarian survey (1993), social assistance included several scores of programs (no fewer than 34 programs are included in the social assistance variable for Hungary). The most important were allowance for the third child (known by its Hungarian acronym *GYET*), and income supplement for the long-term unemployed. Payment for both was linked to the minimum pension (see World Bank, 1996d, Box 2.1, p. 27). There are also numerous locally funded and administered programs that often use their own eligibility criteria.[9] In almost all programs, however, either the eligibility criterion or the amount of the benefit is linked to the minimum pension.[10] The minimum pension was also the best-known "national anchor" and was either explicitly or implicitly used as a guide by local social assistance offices. We therefore use the minimum pension—which, on average in 1993, amounted to Ft. 6,400 ($70) per month—as the poverty line.

*The poor.* Of all households, 7.5 percent had per capita expenditures lower than the poverty threshold; 7.3 percent of households were

**Table 3.3.    Hungary: Who receives social assistance?**

|  | Total | Eligible for assistance (expenditure-poor) | Not eligible for assistance (non-poor) |
|---|---|---|---|
| All households | 100 | 7.5 | 92.5 |
| Receiving SA | 24.4 | 3.2 | 21.2 |
| Income-poor | 7.3 | 3.2 | 4.1 |
| | | | |
| Receiving SA | 100 | 13.3 | 86.7 |

|  |  | Receiving assistance | Not receiving assistance |
|---|---|---|---|
| All poor | 100 | 43.4 | 56.6 |
| Hard-core poor | 100 | 48.9 | 51.1 |
| All non-poor | 100 | 22.9 | 77.1 |

*Note*: Hard-core poor are defined as both income- and expenditure-poor. SA = social assistance.

income-poor, and only 3.2 percent of households were both expenditure- and income-poor (see Table 3.3).[11] The poverty threshold was equal to 55 percent of average per capita expenditure. As before, the term "poor" is used only for the expenditure-poor.

*Who are the recipients of social assistance?* Figure 3.6 illustrates where along the income distribution spectrum were the household recipients of social assistance. Each dot in this and subsequent figures represents the mean value for each percentile (81 households) of welfare distribution, going from the poorest (the first percentile) to the richest (the one hundredth percentile).

Overall an extremely high 24.4 percent of households report receiving some social assistance (see the horizontal line drawn at y = 24.4 in Figure 3.6). The percentage of recipients is high among both the poor and non-poor: among the poor, 43 percent were recipients of social assistance, among the non-poor, 23 percent (Table 3.3). Hard-core poor—that is, households that were both income- and expenditure-poor—have a somewhat higher probability of receiving assistance (49 percent) than the rest of the poor. As in Poland, the share of recipients (or differently put, the probability of receipt of

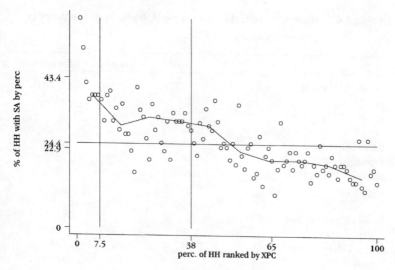

Note: Mean calculated across households.

**Figure 3.6. Hungary: Percentage of household recipients of social assistance by level of welfare (expenditure per capita)**

social assistance) clearly declines with the level of welfare (Figure 3.6). Among the poorest, the likelihood of receiving social assistance exceeds one-half; among the richest, the probability is less, but never below 10 percent—which is a very high percentage.[12]

The leakage in terms of households is almost 87 percent (see Table 3.3) and in terms of money is 77 percent (Table 3.4).

Note that while the slope of the line in Figure 3.6 is similar to that for Poland, the quadrants (and particularly the two empty quadrants) are not as strongly delineated. In particular, if in Figure 3.6 we draw a line at x = 38, thus making the percentage of the poor (eligible for social assistance) the same as in Poland, the households between the thirty-eighth and sixty-fifth percentile whose probability of receipt of social assistance in Poland is below-average have, in Hungary, an around average probability. These households (the "middle class") are consequently the main gainers compared to Poland.

**Table 3.4.    Hungary: Social assistance—Reduction of the poverty gap and leakage**

|  | Total | The poor | The non-poor |
|---|---|---|---|
| Social assistance (Ft. million) | 3.129 | 0.716 | 2.413 |
|  | (100) | (22.9) | (77.1) |
|  |  |  |  |
| In million forints p.m. |  |  |  |
| Expenditures | 71.712 | 12.342 | 259.370 |
| Expenditure of those with SA > 0 | 66.997 | 5.701 | 61.296 |
| Income | 259.646 | 36.135 | 223.511 |
| Poverty gap | 3.076 | 3.076 | 0 |
|  |  |  |  |
| Social assistance as percentage of |  |  |  |
| Expenditures | 1.1 | 5.8 | 0.9 |
| Expenditure of those with SA > 0 | 4.7 | 12.6 | 3.9 |
| Income | 1.4 | 3.1 | 0.9 |
| poverty gap | 101.7 | 23.3 | — |
|  |  |  |  |
| Social assistance per recipient household |  |  |  |
| (Ft/$ p.m.) a/ | 1580 ($17) | 2719 ($30) | 1406 ($15) |
| Expenditure per capita of those *with* |  |  |  |
| social assistance ($ p.m.) a/ | $123 | $55 | $134 |
| *Memo*: Expenditure per capita (overall |  |  |  |
| average $ p.m.) a/ | $139 | $57 | $147 |
| HH size (overall average) | 2.8 | 4.0 | 2.7 |

*Note*: In average 1993 prices. Exchange rate: Ft. 92 = $1. p.m. = per month. SA = social assistance. HH = household.
a/ Mean across households

*How much do they get?* Figure 3.7 shows the average amounts of social assistance (in forint per month) received by each percentile. The overall average amount of social assistance was Ft. 367, or $4 per household per month, with Ft. 1,145 ($12) among the poor and Ft. 307 ($3) among the non-poor. The average amount of assistance received by the *recipient* household was $17. Among the poor, the average amount was $30, among the non-poor $15. The poor also had about two times greater probability of receiving social assistance (43 vs. 23 percent) than the non-poor.[13]

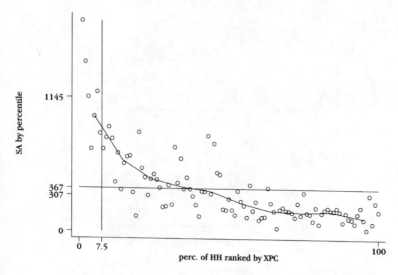

*Note*: Mean calculated across households.

**Figure 3.7. Hungary: Amounts of received social assistance (in Ft per household per month) by level of welfare (expenditure per capita)**

Among the poor, social assistance recipients were not, on a per capita basis, significantly poorer than those who did not receive assistance (per capita expenditures of, respectively, $55 and $57; see Table 3.4). Among the non-poor, the recipients were, on average, 10 percent poorer than the non-recipients ($134 vs. $147).

*How much of the poverty gap is closed by social assistance?* The total monthly expenditure-based poverty gap calculated from the 1993 *Household Budget Survey* was Ft. 3.1 million as compared to total monthly household expenditures of Ft. 271.7 million or income of Ft. 259.6 million (Table 3.4). Thus, to close the entire poverty gap one would need to transfer to the poor and to the poor only about 1.1 percent of total expenditures. Total social assistance (in the sample) was exactly Ft. 3.1 million. Social assistance spending thus covered the entire poverty gap. However, out of that amount, only Ft. 0.7 million was transferred to the poor, while the rest was paid out

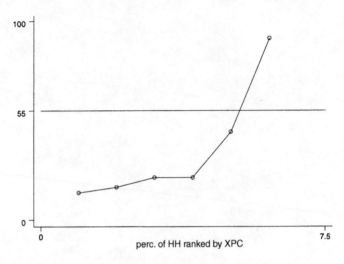

*Note*: Mean calculated across households.

**Figure 3.8. Hungary: Social assistance received as percentage of the poverty gap by level of welfare (expenditures per capita)**

to the non-poor, thus yielding a leakage of more than three-fourths. The well-targeted social assistance therefore eliminated 23.3 percent of the expenditure-based poverty gap.

As can be seen from Figure 3.8, the social assistance-to-poverty gap ratio steadily rises as we move further from the poorest households. Among the households that are at the "edge" of poverty (i.e., around the seventh percentile) social assistance closes almost the entire poverty gap. On average, the (household-weighted) social assistance/poverty gap ratio was 55 percent.[14]

*How much of total expenditures is financed out of social assistance?* On average, social assistance accounted for 1.5 percent of total expenditures (averaged across households; see Figure 3.9) or 1.1 percent in money terms (see Table 3.4). Among the poor, social assistance "pays" for 5.8 percent of their expenditures, among the rich for less than 1 percent. Looking only at those who receive social assistance, it covers 4.7 percent of their expenditures with almost 13

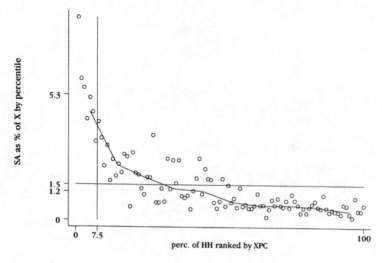

Note: Mean calculated across households.

**Figure 3.9. Hungary: Social assistance as a percentage of expenditures by level of welfare**

percent among the poor households and almost 4 percent among the non-poor (Table 3.4).

*The poor who do not receive social assistance.* Overall, 56.6 percent of the poor receive no social assistance (see Table 3.3 and Figure 3.10). The percentage of the *excluded* poor declines rather sharply as one moves (leftward) toward the poorer households (see Figure 3.10), a fact that, as in Poland, suggests that delivery of social assistance improves with the depth of poverty.

## C.  Bulgaria

*Eligibility for social assistance.* At the time of the household budget survey (January to June 1995), social assistance eligibility was based on the "guaranteed minimum income," a basket of 22 goods defined in 1991 and whose value was periodically, but not automatically,

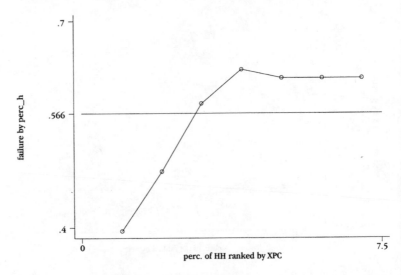

*Note*: Mean calculated across households.

**Figure 3.10. Hungary: Failure to deliver social assistance (share of the poor who do not receive social assistance)**

adjusted for inflation. The value of the basket was lev 1,325 ($20) for the first quarter of 1995, and lev 1,500 ($23) for the second. This gives the first semester value of lev 1,412 ($21). The amount of the "guaranteed minimum income" by household was officially calculated as follows: for the first adult member 100 percent of the value of the basket, for the second and all subsequent adults 80 percent of the value of the basket, and for each child (under 14 years of age) 40 percent of the value. This represents also our "poverty line."

*The poor*. Only 2.1 percent of households had expenditures below the poverty threshold (see the line drawn at x = 3 in Figure 3.11), while 6 percent were income-poor. Only 1.1 percent of households were both income- and expenditure-poor (Table 3.5).[15] The small percentage of those eligible for social assistance clearly implies that, unlike in Poland and Hungary, the poverty threshold was very austere: it was equal to 27 percent of mean expenditures.[16]

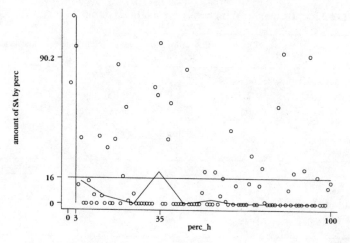

Note: Mean calculated across households.

**Figure 3.11. Bulgaria: Amounts of received social assistance (in Lev per household per month) by level of welfare (expenditure per capita)**

*Who are the recipients of social assistance?* The percentage of people who report receiving some social assistance was similarly small: only 2.55 percent of the population. Moreover, there was not much overlap between the poor and those who were receiving social assistance: only 8 percent of the all social assistance recipients were poor—that is, theoretically eligible to receive social assistance. Social assistance paid out to the remaining 92 percent of households was, therefore, leakage (see Table 3.5). The probability of a poor household receiving assistance was 9.6 percent vs. the probability of a rich household of only 2.4 percent.

*How much do they get?* The average amount of social assistance received (including in the calculations the almost 97.5 percent of the households who received nothing) was lev 16 (about 24 cents) per household per month (see the line drawn at y = 16).[17] The rich have on average received close to nothing, and the poor about lev 90 ($1.50). Figure 3.11 shows that the average amounts are very close

**Table 3.5.   Bulgaria: Who receives social assistance?**

|  | Total | Eligible for assistance (expenditure-poor) | Not eligible for assistance (non-poor) |
|---|---|---|---|
| All households | 100 | 2.1 | 97.9 |
| Receiving SA | 2.55 | 0.2 | 2.35 |
| Income-poor | 6.0 | 1.1 | 4.9 |
| Receiving SA | 100 | 8.0 | 92.0 |
|  | Receiving assistance | Not receiving assistance |  |
| All poor | 100 | 9.6 | 90.4 |
| Hard-core poor | 100 | 7.7 | 92.3 |
| All non-poor | 100 | 2.4 | 97.6 |

*Note*: Hard-core poor are defined as both income and expenditure-poor. SA = social assistance.

to zero for the entire distribution with the exception of the poor (the lowest 3 percent of the population) and the sudden "spike" around the thirty-fifth percentile.

These very small numbers reflect not only small amounts of social assistance paid out but also the fact that very few households received it. As Table 3.6 shows, the average monthly social assistance *per recipient household* was about $14 per month among the poor and $9 among the non-poor with an overall average of about $10.

*How much of the poverty gap is closed by social assistance?* Total expenditure-based monthly poverty gap calculated from the *Survey* was lev 0.114 million as compared to total monthly expenditures of lev 36.5 million or income of 29.4 million (Table 3.6). Thus, to close the entire poverty gap, a mere 0.3 percent of total expenditures would have sufficed. Still, total social assistance fell short of that very modest amount: it was lev 0.039 million, about a third of the poverty gap. Out of the lev 0.395 million disbursed for social assistance, less than lev 0.005 million was paid to the poor, eliminating some 4 percent of the poverty gap. The rest, some 88 percent of social assistance, leaked to the non-poor.

**Table 3.6. Bulgaria: Social assistance—Reduction of the poverty gap and leakage**

|  | Total | The poor | The non-poor |
|---|---|---|---|
| Social assistance (000 lev) | 39.575 | 4.691 | 34.883 |
|  | (100) | (11.9) | (88.1) |
| **In million lev p.m.** |  |  |  |
| Expenditures | 36.513 | 0.202 | 36.311 |
| Expenditure of those with SA > 0 | 0.972 | 0.017 | 0.954 |
| Income | 29.444 | 0.284 | 29.160 |
| Poverty gap | 0.114 | 0.114 | 0 |
| **Social assistance as percentage of** |  |  |  |
| Expenditures | 0.11 | 2.3 | 0.1 |
| Expenditure of those with SA > 0 | 4.1 | 27.6 | 3.7 |
| Income | 0.14 | 1.7 | 0.1 |
| Poverty gap | 34.7 | 4.1 | — |
| Social assistance per recipient household (lev/$ p.m.) | 629 ($10) | 938 ($14) | 601($9) |
| Expenditure per capita of those *with* social assistance ($ p.m.) a/ | $76 | $11 | $81 |
| *Memo*: Expenditure per capita (overall average $ p.m.) a/ | $83 | $14 | $84 |
| HH size (overall average) | 2.92 | 4.3 | 2.89 |

a/ Mean across households. SA = social assistance. HH = household. Leva converted at average first semester 1995 exchange rate (lev 66.123 = $1).

*How much of total expenditures is financed out of social assistance?* On average, social assistance accounted for two-tenths of 1 percent of total expenditures (averaged across households; see Figure 3.12) or 0.11 percent in money terms (see Table 3.6). Among the poor, social assistance pays for 2.3 percent of expenditures; among the rich it is negligible. Finally, for those who are recipients of social assistance, it covers about 4 percent of their expenditures with the proportion rising to almost 28 percent among the poor (Table 3.6). Thus, even if both the amounts and frequency of social assistance are small in overall terms, for the poorest 3 percent of the population,

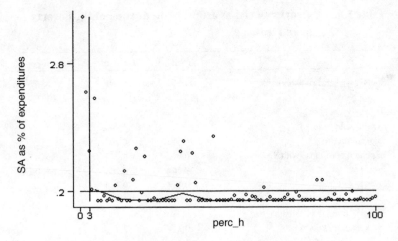

Note: Mean calculated across households.

**Figure 3.12. Bulgaria: Social assistance as percentage of expenditures by level of welfare**

social assistance does provide a certain cushion, financing more than a quarter of their expenditures.

## D.  Estonia

*Eligibility for social assistance.* At the time of the Estonian survey (the third quarter of 1995, all data expressed in July 1995 prices), a household would, in principle, be qualified for social assistance if its monthly per capita income was less than EEK 320 ($29).[18] This poverty line was equal to 39 percent of average monthly per capita expenditures.

*The poor.* The relatively low level of the poverty threshold implied that few households qualified for social assistance: only 8.1 percent of households were income-poor, and 2.8 percent were expenditure-poor (see Table 3.7). Only 1.3 percent of households were both income- and expenditure-poor.[19] As before, we treat the expenditure-poor as "the poor."[20]

**Table 3.7.  Estonia: Who receives social assistance?**

|                | Total | Eligible for assistance (expenditure-poor) | Not eligible for assistance (non-poor) |
|----------------|-------|--------------------------------------------|----------------------------------------|
| All households | 100   | 2.8                                        | 97.2                                   |
| Receiving SA   | 2.7   | 0.3                                        | 2.4                                    |
| Income-poor    | 8.1   | 1.3                                        | 6.8                                    |
| Receiving SA   | 100   | 15.9                                       | 84.1                                   |

|                | | Receiving assistance | Not receiving assistance |
|----------------|-----|----------------------|--------------------------|
| All poor       | 100 | 10.3                 | 89.7                     |
| Hard-core poor | 100 | 15.3                 | 84.7                     |
| All non-poor   | 100 | 2.4                  | 97.6                     |

*Note*: Hard-core poor are defined as both income- and expenditure-poor.
SA = social assistance.

*Who are the recipients?* Figure 3.13 illustrates where along the income distribution spectrum were the recipients of social assistance.[21] Of all households, 2.7 percent report receiving social assistance (based on unweighted sample, the percentage of recipients is 3.6; see the horizontal line in Figure 3.13). Among the poor, the share of social assistance recipients is 10.3 percent; among the non-poor, 2.4 percent (Table 3.1). The share of recipients (or differently put, the probability of receipt of social assistance) declines with level of welfare (Figure 3.13) except for a sudden peak around the sixty-fifth percentile.

All households to the right of the x = 4 line in Figure 3.13 are non-poor and should not in principle receive social assistance. Everything to the right of that line is therefore leakage. In terms of the number of recipients, 84 percent of them are not qualified (see Table 3.7). In terms of money amounts, 88 percent of social assistance leaks (Table 3.8).

*How much do they get?* Figure 3.14 shows the average amounts of social assistance in Estonian crowns (EEK) received by each per-

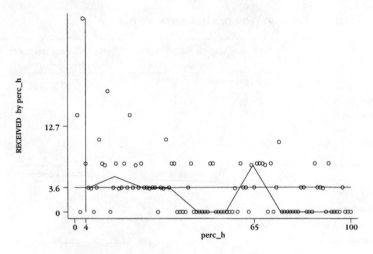

*Note*: Mean calculated across households.

**Figure 3.13. Estonia: Percentage of household recipients of social assistance by level of welfare (expenditure per capita)**

centile. It was about EEK 14 (see horizontal line in Figure 3.14)[22] or slightly more than $1 per household per month on average, but EEK 53 (almost $5) among the poor and EEK 14 ($1.1) among the non-poor. The average amount of assistance per recipient household was about $33 per month (Table 3.8). Among the poor, the average amount was $36, among the non-poor $33. The difference between the poor and non-poor in terms of access to social assistance is not due to the amounts they received, but in the probability of receiving it. The probability of the poor receiving social assistance was four times higher than that of the non-poor (10.3 percent vs. 2.4 percent), but the amounts received were almost equal.[23]

*How much of the poverty gap is closed by social assistance?* Total monthly expenditure-based poverty gap calculated from the *Survey* is EEK 17,700 as compared to total monthly expenditures of EEK 7.158 million or income of EEK 6.885 million (Table 3.7). Thus, to close the entire poverty gap one would need to transfer to

**Table 3.8.  Estonia: Social assistance—Reduction of the poverty gap and leakage**

|  | Total | The poor | The non-poor |
|---|---|---|---|
| Social assistance (EEK 000) | 27.455 | 3.28 | 24.175 |
|  | (100) | (11.9) | (88.1) |
|  |  |  |  |
| In '000 EEK p.m. |  |  |  |
| Expenditures | 7157.776 | 62.482 | 7713.294 |
| Expenditure of those with SA > 0 | 185.29 | 7.897 | 177.393 |
| Income | 6885.64 | 95.215 | 6790.425 |
| Poverty gap | 17.697 | 17.697 | 0 |
|  |  |  |  |
| Social assistance as percentage of |  |  |  |
| Expenditures | 0.38 | 5.2 | 0.31 |
| Expenditure of those with SA > 0 | 14.8 | 41.5 | 13.6 |
| Income | 0.40 | 3.4 | 0.36 |
| Poverty gap | 155.1 | 18.5 | — |
|  |  |  |  |
| Social assistance per recipient |  |  |  |
| household (EEK/ $ p.m.) | 367 ($33) | 400 ($36) | 363 ($33) |
| Expenditure per capita of those *with* |  |  |  |
| social assistance ($ p.m.) a/ | $76 | $23 | $83 |
| *Memo*: Expenditure per capita |  |  |  |
| (overall average $ p.m.) a/ | $102 | $23 | $104 |
| HH size (overall average) | 3.11 | 4.15 | 3.07 |

*Note*: In July 1995 prices. Exchange rate: EEK 11.1 = $1. p.m. = per month. SA = social assistance. HH = household.
a/ Mean across households.

the poor, and to the poor only, a mere 0.2 percent of total population expenditures. Such a small amount of the poverty gap is a reflection of a very austere poverty line (the poverty gap, in terms of total expenditures, is about the same as in Bulgaria). Total social assistance (in the sample) amounted to EEK 27,455 or in excess of one and one-half times the poverty gap. However, only 12 percent of that amount was paid to the poor, therefore "covering" only 18 percent of the poverty gap. If we look at the average

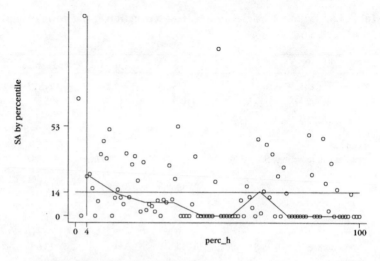

Note: Mean calculated across households.

Figure 3.14. Estonia: Amounts of received social assistance (in EEK per household per month) by level of welfare (expenditure per capita)

social-assistance-to-poverty-gap ratio across households as in Figure 3.15 rather than at the overall money values, the ratio is 42 percent.[24]

*How much of total expenditures is financed out of social assistance?* On average, social assistance accounted for 0.7 percent of total expenditures (averaged across households; see Figure 3.16) or less than 0.4 percent in money terms (see Table 3.8). Among the poor, social assistance paid for 5.2 percent of expenditures; among the non-poor, it was negligible (0.3 percent of expenditures). For the recipient households, however, social assistance covered about 15 percent of expenditures, and for poor recipients much more: 41.5 percent (Table 3.8).

The big difference between the share of social assistance in overall average expenditures (less than 0.4 percent) and in expenditures

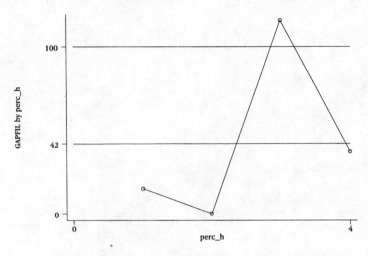

Note: Mean calculated across households.

**Figure 3.15. Estonia: Social assistance received as percentage of the poverty gap by level of welfare (expenditures per capita)**

of recipients (15 percent) indicates that social assistance was distributed in relatively large chunks and to few people. And indeed, the average recipient household in Estonia received twice as much as the average recipient household in Hungary ($33 vs. $17)—and yet the overall social assistance spending in Estonia was 0.4 percent of expenditures vs. 1.4 percent in Hungary. As we shall see in the next section, Estonia's social assistance can be considered "concentrated."

*The poor who do not receive social assistance.* Overall, 90 percent of the poor received no social assistance. The percentage of the excluded seems to decrease with welfare—that is, as one moves toward the less poor (see Figure 3.17)—but that can hardly be considered a regularity in view of the very small number of the people who are eligible for social assistance.

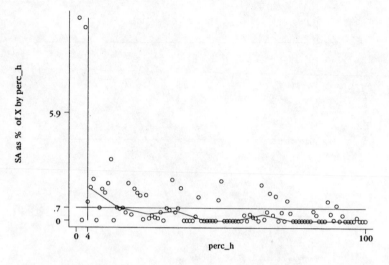

*Note*: Mean calculated across households.

**Figure 3.16. Estonia: Social assistance as a percentage of the expenditures by level of welfare**

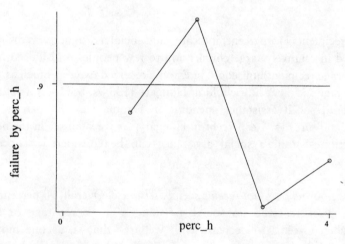

*Note*: Mean calculated across households.

**Figure 3.17. Estonia: Failure to deliver social assistance (share of the poor who do not receive social assistance)**

## E.  Russia

*Eligibility for social assistance.* At the time the survey was conducted, from October 1993 to February 1994, the official average per capita poverty line for the entire population (as opposed, e.g., to the elderly, children) was Rb. 37,900 ($32).[25] This is the average all-Russia subsistence minimum as originally calculated by the Ministry of Labor and adopted by the government in November 1992. It is updated monthly in line with consumer price inflation. Obviously, given the vastness of the country and the differences in socioeconomic conditions, the effectively used (applied) poverty threshold lines differed not only between the oblasts but even within the same oblasts. The social assistance system in Russia, like that in Hungary, is very decentralized, partly because some decentralization is inevitable in a huge country, partly out of necessity (lack of funds in many regions).[26] The poverty line of Rb. 37,900 per capita was equal to 65 percent of average monthly per capita expenditures, placing Russia among the countries with high poverty lines.

*The poor.* A total of 36.1 percent of households had per capita expenditures below the poverty threshold; 57.3 percent of households had income per capita below the threshold (Table 3.9). As shown in Table 3.9, almost 30 percent of the households were both expenditure- and income-poor. The correlation between expenditure-poor (POORX) and income-poor (POORY) was 0.34; the correlation between per capita expenditures and income was 0.48. The latter is with Bulgaria the lowest correlation among all countries and suggests a severe underestimation of incomes (a point that was often made with respect to Russia).[27] As before, we treat the expenditure-poor as "the poor."

*Who are the recipients?* Figure 3.18 illustrates where along the income distribution curve are the households that are recipients of social assistance.[28] Thirteen percent of households received some form of social assistance from local authorities (see the horizontal line drawn at y = 13 in Figure 3.18). There was almost no difference

**Table 3.9.    Russia: Who receives social assistance?**

|  | Total | Eligible for assistance (expenditure-poor) | Not eligible for assistance (non-poor) |
|---|---|---|---|
| All households | 100 | 36.1 | 63.9 |
| Receiving SA | 13.0 | 4.6 | 8.4 |
| Income-poor | 57.3 | 28.8 | 28.5 |
| Receiving SA | 100 | 35.4 | 64.6 |
|  |  | Receiving assistance | Not receiving assistance |
| All poor | 100 | 12.7 | 87.3 |
| Hard-core poor | 100 | 11.8 | 88.2 |
| All non-poor | 100 | 13.1 | 86.9 |

*Note*: Hard-core poor are defined as both income- and expenditure-poor. SA = social assistance.

between the poor and non-poor: among the poor, 12.7 percent of households were recipients; among the non-poor, slightly more (13.1 percent).

All households to the right of the x = 37 line, the non-poor, should not—in principle—be eligible for social assistance. In effect, almost two-thirds of the total number of recipients (64.6 percent) do not qualify for social assistance (see Table 3.9). Since the average amounts paid out across income distribution, and thus to the poor and non-poor, are very similar (Figure 3.19), the leakage in monetary terms is likewise almost two-thirds of the total amount spent (see Table 3.10).

*How much do they get?* Figure 3.19 shows the average amounts of social assistance (in roubles per month) received by each percentile. The average amount was Rb. 715, or only 60 cents per household per month, with no difference between the poor and non-poor. Since we know that 13 percent of households were recipients of social assistance, we readily calculate that the average amount of assistance given was less than $5 per household. This is the lowest amount among all the countries considered here. The average

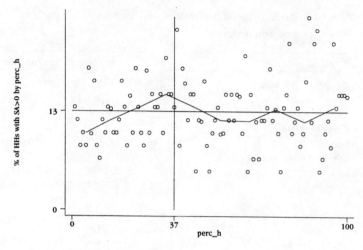

Note: Mean calculated across households.

Figure 3.18. Russia: Percentage of households recipients of social assistance by level of welfare (expenditures per capita)

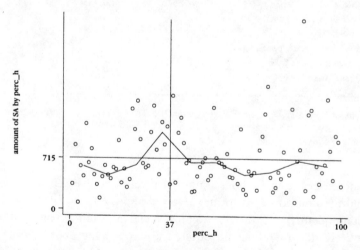

Note: Mean calculated across households.

Figure 3.19. Russia: Amounts of received social assistance (in roubles per household per month) by level of welfare (expenditures per capita)

**Table 3.10.  Russia: Social assistance—Reduction of the poverty gap and leakage**

|  | Total | The poor | The non-poor |
|---|---|---|---|
| Social assistance (Rb. million) | 4.227 | 1.522 | 2.705 |
|  | (100) | (36.0) | (64.0) |
| In million roubles p.m. |  |  |  |
| Expenditures | 945.596 | 141.677 | 803.918 |
| Expenditure of those with SA > 0 | 119.301 | 18.374 | 100.928 |
| Income | 630.577 | 152.079 | 478.498 |
| Poverty gap | 102.261 | 102.261 | 0 |
| Social assistance as percentage of |  |  |  |
|   Expenditures | 0.45 | 1.1 | 0.34 |
|   Expenditure of those with SA > 0 | 3.5 | 8.3 | 2.7 |
|   Income | 0.67 | 1.0 | 0.56 |
|   Poverty gap | 4.1 | 1.5 | — |
| Social assistance per recipient |  |  |  |
|   household (Rb/$ p.m.) | 5518 ($5) | 5616 ($5) | 5465 ($4.5) |
| Expenditure per capita of those *with* |  |  |  |
|   social assistance ($ p.m.) a/ | $54 | $19 | $72 |
| *Memo*: Expenditure per capita |  |  |  |
|   (overall average $ p.m.) a/ | $52 | $19 | $71 |
| HH size (overall average) | 2.75 | 3.02 | 2.61 |

*Note*: In November 1993 prices. Exchange rate: Rb. 1,194 = $1. p.m. = per month. SA = social assistance. HH = household.
a/ Mean across households.

amount per recipient household varied very little between the poor and the non-poor: the former received about $5, the latter $4.50. Consequently, the distribution of social assistance was almost entirely flat: there was no difference between the poor and non-poor in terms of probability of access to social assistance, nor in the amounts disbursed.

*How much of the poverty gap is covered by social assistance?* The total monthly expenditure-based poverty gap calculated from the

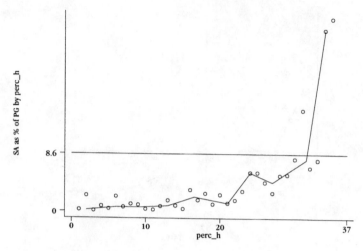

Note: Mean calculated across households.

**Figure 3.20. Russia: Social assistance received as percentage of the poverty gap by level of welfare (expenditure per capita)**

Russian *Survey* was Rb. 102.2 billion as compared to total monthly expenditures of Rb. 945.6 billion, or income of Rb. 630.6 billion (Table 3.10). Thus, to close the entire poverty gap one would need to transfer to the poor, and to the poor only, almost 11 percent of total population expenditures. This is, together with Poland, the largest gap of all countries. Total social assistance (in the sample) amounted to Rb. 4.2 billion, or only 4.1 percent of the poverty gap. Only Rb. 1.5 billion was paid out to the poor, thus "covering" 1.5 percent of the expenditure-based poverty gap.

If we look at the average social-assistance-to-poverty-gap ratio across households as in Figure 3.20 rather than at the overall money values, we find that social assistance covered 8.6 percent of the poverty gap. The coverage increases strongly as households become less poor. Thus less than 1 percent of poverty gap is eliminated among the poorest decile households while almost 40 percent of the poverty gap is eliminated among the households belonging to the fourth decile. This is, of course, a feature observed in all the countries here.

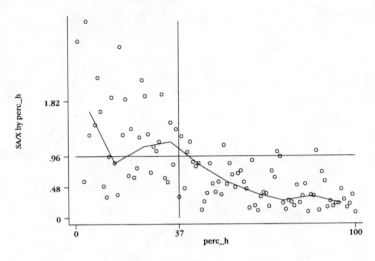

Note: Mean calculated across households.

**Figure 3.21. Russia: Social assistance received as percentage of expenditures by level of welfare (expenditure per capita)**

*How much of total expenditures is financed out of social assistance?* On average, social assistance accounts for about 1 percent of total expenditures (averaged across households; see Figure 3.21) or 0.45 percent in money terms (see Table 3.10). Among the poor, social assistance pays for 1 percent of expenditures, among the rich for one-third a percent only.

*The poor who do not receive social assistance.* Overall, 87 percent of the poor receive no social assistance. The percentage of the excluded poor declines as one moves toward the *less* poor, those closer to the poverty threshold (see Figure 3.22), which indicates a weakness in the targeting of social assistance. This is a feature that Russia shares with Estonia, while in Poland and Hungary the failure to deliver increases with level of welfare (see the positively sloped line in Figures 3.5 and 3.10).

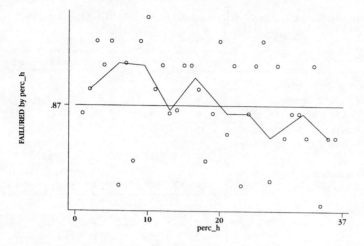

**Figure 3.22. Russia: Failure to deliver social assistance (share of the poor who do not receive social assistance)**

## 3.2. COMPARING THE PERFORMANCE AND FEATURES OF SOCIAL ASSISTANCE POLICIES

### A.   *The Performance: Assessing Efficiency and Effectiveness*

Comparing the performance of social policies is difficult even when maximum effort is made to make the household data comparable. There is—once the data are made broadly comparable—at least one additional adjustment to be made. As we have seen in Section 1, the countries' effective poverty lines differ a lot in terms of their relative value, that is, compared to the average expenditure or income of the country. Poland, Russia, and Hungary have relatively high poverty lines, equal to, respectively, 77, 65 and 55 percent of average per capita expenditures. Estonia and Bulgaria have relatively low poverty lines, 28 and 39 percent of average per capita expenditures (see row 5, Table 3.11). When the poverty lines are so vastly differ-

**Table 3.11.   Characteristics and performance of social assistance systems**

|  | Bulgaria | Estonia | Poland | Russia | Hungary |
|---|---|---|---|---|---|
| **System characteristics** | | | | | |
| (1) % of HHs receiving SA | 2.55 | 2.7 | 3.7 | 13.0 | 24.4 |
| (2) SA as % of expenditures | 0.11 | 0.38 | 0.74 | 0.45 | 1.1 |
| (3) SA per recipient HH ($ pm) | 10 | 33 | 54 | 5 | 17 |
| (4) SA as % of expend. of recipient HHs | 4.1 | 14.8 | 22.1 | 3.5 | 4.7 |
| (5) Eligibility threshold as % of mean per capita expenditures | 28 | 39 | 77 | 65 | 55 |
| **System performance** | | | | | |
| (6) % of SA received by the lowest decile | 22.3 | 34.7 | 20.5 | 8.2 | 27.2 |
| (7) SA to the bottom decile as % of the poverty gap a/ | 1.3 | 7.0 | 9.4 | 3.3 | 28.8 |
| **Overall expenditures and distribution** | | | | | |
| (8) Poverty gap of the lowest decile as % of all expenditures | 1.9 | 2.1 | 1.6 | 1.0 | 1.1 |
| (9) *Memo*: Overall expenditure (income) per capita in $ pm b/ | 83 (67) | 74 (71) | 93 (99) | 47 (32) | 134 (128) |
| (10) Gini coefficient of expenditures (income) per capita (individual-based) | 28.6 (31.4) | 30.7 (35.4) | 27.4 (29.1) | 40.1 (44.5) | 22.8 (21.8) |

*Note*: Countries ranked from left to right according to the percentage of households who are receiving social assistance. SA = social assistance. HH = household. p.m. = per month.
a/ Poverty gap of the lowest decile. The poverty gap is expenditure-based (after social assistance).
b/ Household-weighted.

ent, comparing the performance of the system—looking at the leakage to those above the poverty line—is meaningless. With a poverty line of, say, twice the average per capita expenditures, there would be almost no leakage. But it would not guarantee that the money went to the truly needy.

Thus, the adjustment we ought to make in order to judge the efficiency of social assistance is to standardize: to look, for example, at how much money is disbursed to the bottom decile. We thereby (arbi-

**Table 3.12.   Comparing the performance of the social assistance systems**

|  | Hungary | Estonia | Poland | Bulgaria | Russia |
|---|---|---|---|---|---|
| Efficiency: % of SA received by the lowest decile | 27.2 | 34.7 | 20.5 | 22.3 | 8.2 |
| Effectiveness: SA as % of the poverty gap of the lowest decile | 28.8 | 7.0 | 9.4 | 1.3 | 3.3 |
| Relative effectiveness | 26.2 | 18.3 | 12.6 | 11.4 | 7.3 |
| Correlation btw. SAPC and perc_h | −0.13 | −0.04 | −0.06 | −0.03 | +0.03 |
| Concentration coefficient a/ | −25.8 | −16.2 | −19.8 | −13.8 | +8.2 |

*Note*: Relative effectiveness is calculated as the ratio between effectiveness, and social assistance as percentage of total expenditures. Countries are ranked from left to right according to relative effectiveness. SA = social assistance. SAPC = social assistance per capita. perc_h = percentiles of households formed according the household per capita expenditures. a/ The concentration coefficient captures both inherent inequality with which a given income source is distributed (source Gini coefficient) and the correlation of that source with the overall income. Thus, an inherently unequal source like social assistance with a high Gini coefficient will have a low or negative correlation with overall income (because most of social assistance recipients are poor), and its concentration coefficient will be low or negative. The exact definition of the concentration coefficient of the source $i$ is $C_i = G_i R_i$ where $G_i$ = Gini coefficient of the source and $R_i$ = [cov($i$, rank(income))]/[cov ($i$, rank($i$))] ratio of covariances between source $i$ and ranking of recipients according to total income, and source $i$ and ranking of recipients according to source $i$. *rank (.)* is a rank function taking values from 1 to N (total number of recipients). If the two ranks coincide, R = 1, and Cw = Gw. Since in cov[$i$,rank($i$)] both $i$ and *rank(i)* uniformly increase, its value will be greater or equal than that of cov[$i$, rank(income)]. Therefore, R ≤ 1.

trarily, but not unreasonably) assume that the objective of welfare policy is to help the poorest 10 percent of the population. We show, in row 6 (Table 3.11), the percentage of total social assistance disbursed to the bottom decile: it lies between 20 and 27 percent in Poland, Hungary, and Bulgaria, and 35 percent in Estonia. Russia is an outlier, with only 8 percent reaching the lowest decile. Efficiency, which is measured by the share of all money going to the target group, is consequently the highest in Estonia and the lowest in Russia (see Table 3.12).

But in addition, we must look at the effectiveness of social assistance: what percentage of the poverty gap does social assistance cover?[29] Now—unlike in the case of efficiency—the overall *amount* of social assistance (relative to total expenditures or income) matters as well. Clearly, if two countries have the same poverty gap and pattern of social assistance spending, directing to the lowest decile, say a quarter of all social assistance, the country that spends more on social assistance will reduce the poverty gap by more. This is reflected in line 7 (Table 3.11). We see that in Hungary, social assistance fills almost 29 percent of the poverty gap of the *lowest decile,* while in Bulgaria, social assistance is equal to only a little more than 1 percent of the gap. The reason lies, of course, in much greater spending in Hungary than in Bulgaria. Hungary's social assistance spending is equal to 1.1 percent of all household expenditures, ten times as much as in Bulgaria (see row 2 in Table 3.12). Judged by the effectiveness of social assistance, Hungary is strongly ahead of all other countries (see Table 3.12).

We can easily multiply the criteria by which to judge the performance of the system of social assistance. In row 3, Table 3.12, we show the *relative* effectiveness defined as the percentage of poverty gap eliminated ( = effectiveness) divided by the spending on social assistance as percentage of total expenditures. This indicator combines the achievements (how much of the poverty gap was reduced?) with costs (how much was spent to achieve this?).[30] According to this criterion, Hungary and Estonia are the best. Russia again shows by far the worst performance. It may be noted that while Russia's and Estonia's social assistance amounts are approximately the same—about 0.4 percent of total household expenditures—the distribution of social assistance is much more widespread in Russia: thirteen percent of households in Russia receive some (meager) social assistance vs. 3 percent of households in Estonia. A flat distribution in Russia—to many people, almost the same (very little) money—results in the fact that *less* than a tenth of social assistance goes to the bottom decile, while in Estonia, the bottom decile gets more than a third of social assistance.

In rows 4 and 5 (Table 3.12), we display two additional criteria with which to assess the quality of social assistance: the correlation coefficient between the amount of social assistance received by each percentile of welfare distribution and percentiles, and the concentration coefficient of social assistance. The more negative the coefficients, the more is social assistance (in absolute amounts) targeted toward the poorest households. According to both coefficients, Hungary is the best; Russia the worst. Russia is the only country where the concentration coefficient is positive, indicating that social assistance is pro-rich in absolute terms: that is, the non-poor receive more in absolute amounts than do the poor.

## B.  Can We Distinguish Between the Different Systems? An Attempted Classification

The comparison between different countries in Table 3.13 allows us to zero in on the distinguishing characteristics of each system. We select three criteria: the relative level of the poverty line (high/low), the number of recipients (coverage of social assistance: high/low), and the importance of social assistance for the recipient households (high/low). All these indicators are aggregate indicators describing the features of the system (whether overall spending is high or low; whether many or few receive assistance) but *not* its performance. This caveat is important because below we shall try to see if indeed there is a relationship between these aggregate (systemic) features and performance.

Consider Poland and Hungary, which both have relatively high poverty lines. But whereas Hungary's coverage of the population by social assistance is extensive (almost one household in four receives some kind of social assistance), it is very limited in Poland: coverage is less than 4 percent (see row 1 in Table 3.11). Moreover, while in Hungary such widespread assistance results in the fact that, for a recipient household on average, social assistance is not particularly important (it covers only 4.7 percent of recipients' expenditures), in Poland social assistance is indeed important for the recipients: on average it pays for 22 percent of their expenditures (see row 4 in Table 3.11). In dollar terms too, the average disbursement in Poland is relatively high: $54 per household per month vs. $17 in Hungary. Thus, the two systems clearly differ. We describe the Hungarian system as HHL system (*high* poverty line, *high* number of recipients, *low* amount per recipient), and Polish system as HLH

**Table 3.13.   Characteristics of the systems**

|  | Poland | Bulgaria | Hungary | Estonia | Russia |
|---|---|---|---|---|---|
| Poverty line | High | Low | High | Low | High |
| Percentage of recipients | Low | Low | High | Low | High |
| Importance of SA for recipients | High | Low | Low | High | Low |
| Type of system | HLH | LLL | HHL | LLH | HHL |

H/L = level of poverty line: high/low (over/under 50 percent of average expenditures). H/L = many or few receive SA (under/over 10 percent of the population). H/L = Social assistance (SA) is important (high) or not (low) (under/over 10 percent of recipients' expenditures).
*Source*: Table 3.11.

(*high* poverty line, *low* number of recipients, *high* amount per recipient). The same analysis is made for the other countries as shown in Table 3.13.

Consider now Poland and Estonia. Despite the difference in the level of their poverty lines, Poland and Estonia share a very important feature: their systems are *concentrated,* which means that the number of recipients is low, but to the *recipients* social assistance is a fairly important source of income (Table 3.14). Hungary, as we have seen, is revealed to be quite different. Its social assistance is *dispersed*: it covers many people, but on average the transfer is small. The situation is the same in Russia. In Bulgaria, social assistance is practically irrelevant: it covers few people and pays them very little. We thus locate each country in one of the four quadrants. The empty

**Table 3.14.   Taxonomy of social assistance: Concentrated, dispersed, and irrelevant social assistance**

|  | Importance of social assistance | |
|---|---|---|
| **Number of recipients** | SA relatively important for recipients | SA relatively unimportant for recipients |
| Low number of recipients | Poland<br>Estonia<br>**[CONCENTRATED]** | Bulgaria<br>    **[IRRELEVANT]** |
| High number of recipients |  | Hungary<br>Russia    **[DISPERSED]** |

SW quadrant would require a very high spending on social assistance: social assistance would need to be disbursed to many and to be important for the recipients. Not surprisingly, no country belongs there.

## C.  Is There a Relationship Between the Type of System and Its Performance?

The previous section looked at the systemic features of social assistance in the five countries. It deliberately excluded the performance characteristics. Table 3.15 presents a classification of the systems based on their targeting performance. The assessment is based on the system's focus on the poorest decile as determined from the efficiency and relative effectiveness measures (rows 1 and 3 in Table 3.12).[31]

There is not much apparent relationship between the classification attempted in Table 3.14 and the performance of the system. Hungary and Russia, both with dispersed systems, have entirely different performances. A possible explanation is that dispersed and decentralized systems (in terms of local funding and decision making) as the Hungarian and Russian are, produce different results depending on whether they operate in a homogeneous country with small differences in regional incomes, or in a very heterogeneous country where income differences are large.

The Russian system became decentralized by default after the breakup of the Soviet Union, and weakening financial role of the central (Russian) government. Since the central government had practically no money to allocate for social assistance, it understand-

**Table 3.15.   Focus on the poorest decile**

| Good focus | Weak focus |
|---|---|
| Hungary | Poland |
| Estonia | Bulgaria |
|  | Russia |

*Note*: Good focus on the poor if percentage of social assistance received by the bottom decile exceeds 25 percent, and if relative effectiveness exceeds 15 (see Table 3.12).

ably could not lay down the terms under which autonomous republics, oblasts, or cities were to distribute social aid. Social assistance thus became entirely a local matter: locally financed, and with benefit eligibility and benefit levels wholly under local control. This also led to a wide dispersion of the coverage and levels of social assistance in the country. The Hungarian system became extremely decentralized at about the same time as the Russian did, following the 1990 *Act on Local Self-Government*. The Act led to the creation of more than 3,200 local councils (in a country of fewer than 10 million people) with an almost full control over social assistance. Local governments disburse two kinds of assistance: regular social assistance and emergency aid. The first is financed by the central government; the second from local governments' sources. But in both cases, the eligibility is determined by the local governments alone even if in theory the decisions on the distribution of regular social assistance should follow central rules. However, as Sipos (1995, p. 3) writes, "There are no county or lower level supervisory bodies of the central Government that would inspect the local governments that have a broad measure of independence in applying the Social Assistance Law and other pieces of national legislation in the field of social assistance" (for the Hungarian system see also Fabian and Straussman, 1994; Sipos, and Toth, 1998, pp. 243–244).

Poland and Estonia, both with concentrated systems, also display important performance differences. Their systems illustrate two different philosophies. Estonia's social assistance is very strongly "residual" (in the sense of Esping-Andersen, 1990). The aid is focused on the poorest only. Poland's system is open to broader segments of society: the eligibility threshold is much higher. As a result, Polish social assistance is not focused very much on the poorest decile: they receive 20 percent of all spending vs. 35 percent in Estonia.

It would seem, therefore, that the performance is not related to the type of the system as defined in Table 3.14. Other underlying factors, such as the differences in the situation (country characteristics) in which a decentralized social assistance operates, or the "welfare philosophy," are apparently more important. We shall see these differences re-emerge in the next section where we try to see what may explain failure to deliver social assistance to the poor.

# 3.3. WHAT EXPLAINS ERRORS OF EXCLUSION?

We have seen that the percentage of the poor who are *not* receiving social assistance ("error of exclusion") varies from 56 percent in Hungary to 94 percent in Poland. However, this variation in the share of the excluded is not very significant in itself because it is a product of very different poverty lines. Different poverty lines (relative to the country's average income or welfare) may make many households eligible for assistance (as in Poland, where 38 percent of households should, in principle, be eligible), or very few (as in Estonia) where an austere poverty line makes less than 5 percent of households eligible. As mentioned before, this difference in relative poverty lines renders comparisons between other indicators of efficiency of social assistance—leakage as percentage of total funds disbursed, for example, or percentage of the poverty gap eliminated—difficult and in some cases misleading.

More important is to try to explain *who* among the poor are left out of the social assistance system and *why*: in other words, what identifiable household characteristics account for their exclusion? Is it the fact that they live in rural areas, own durables (e.g., a car or productive assets), have an able-bodied male living in the household, or have small families? Finding out what these characteristics are should give us (1) a much better perspective on the efficiency of the system of social assistance. For example, if single mothers are systematically discriminated against, that probably means that the system is operating worse than if households with able-bodied males (who might work informally) are systematically excluded. Also, it should allow us to look more carefully for (2) the true causes of exclusion. For example, if farmers are systematically discriminated against, is it because there are no social assistance offices in the countryside or the ones that exist are understaffed, or is it because the allocation of central funds is biased against rural areas?

A country-by-country analysis of (1) and (2) allows us to better contrast the performance of different countries' systems. In this section, we shall try to identify, using econometric analysis applied to individual data from the five countries, the factors that explain discrimination against (and its obverse, "discrimination in favor") of certain types of households.

## A.  Methodology

We want to estimate econometrically what household characteristics are associated with errors of exclusion. We cannot estimate such regressions simply across *all* households because for the non-poor we cannot, by definition, observe errors of exclusion. We deal with a censored sample. Differently, to run the regressions across the poor households only would yield biased estimates because people are not poor or non-poor randomly. Distinct characteristics (see Chapter 2) are associated with poverty. If that is the case, then, running the regression across the subsample of the poor would be tantamount to disregarding information from the entire sample, thus yielding biased estimates. For example, we might find—when running the regression across the poor only—that the failure to deliver social assistance is strongly related to living in villages (peasants do not get much social assistance). But it could also be that living in a village is a strong determinant of poverty, and once we take it into account, none of the discrimination against peasants per se remains. The same exogeneous variable (living in a village) explains both the poverty status and the error of exclusion. We need to distinguish between the two. To do so, we run a selection model where households first "select" to be in or out of poverty (the so-called "screening" equation). This is a probit regression because the dependent variable takes the value of either 1 or 0 depending on whether the household is, respectively, poor or non-poor. Then, in the second regression, we identify factors that—for the poor households—explain their exclusion from social assistance *controlling* now for the factors that make people more likely to be poor.

We have, in essence, two important econometric problems: the use of a limited dependent variable (binary variable in the first equation), and the selection bias (people "select" to be poor non-randomly). The first problem renders OLS estimators even asymptotically biased; the second problem also makes them biased. We address the selection issue by using the Heckman correction (or Heckman selection model);

we address the limited dependent variable problem by applying the maximum likelihood (ML) estimation. We are thus able to obtain unbiased and asymptotically efficient estimators.[32]

More formally, we observe an error of exclusion only if the household is poor, that is if

$$\beta_1 x_1 + u_1 > 0$$

where $x_1$ is a vector of household characteristics, $\beta_1$ = a vector of coefficients (such as, for example, obtained in Chapter 2) and $u_1$ = a normally distributed random error term. At the same time, there is another equation explaining the exclusion error:

$$FAILURE = \beta_2 x_2 + \sigma u_2$$

where $x_2$ is a vector of household characteristics, $\beta_2$ = a vector of coefficients, $u_2$ = a normally distributed random error term potentially correlated with the first error term ($u_1$) if $\sigma \neq 0$. The two vectors of household characteristics ($x_1$ and $x_2$) must have at least one different variable in order for the two equations to be identified.

Our first ("selection" into poverty) regression is:

(1)    DPOOR = fct (HHSIZE, DEDU1, DEDU2, DEDU3, AGE, AGE$^2$, PRODUCA, DHOUSE, SHRWAGEY, DSEX, DLOC1, DLOC2, DLFS1, DLFS2)

where binary (0–1) variables are prefixed by a *D* standing for dummy variable, and all variables are household-based,

DPOOR = poverty status (poor = 1), where *poor* is defined based on country's official poverty line as in Section 3.1
HHSIZE = household size,
DEDU1 = dummy for primary education or less (of household head),
DEDU2 = dummy for secondary (general) education of household head,

DEDU3 = dummy for secondary vocational or technical education of household head (omitted variable = university education),
AGE = age of the household head,
PRODUCA = ownership of productive assets,
DHOUSE = dummy for tenancy status (vs. home ownership),
SHRWAGEY = share of wage income in total household income (to proxy linkage with labor market),
DSEX = dummy for female-headed household,
DLOC1 = dummy for other cities,
DLOC2 = dummy for rural (omitted variable = capital city),
DLFS1 = dummy if household head is unemployed, and
DLFS2 = dummy if household head is inactive (omitted variable = employed).

Our second ("error of exclusion") regression is:

(2)    FAILURE = fct (HHSIZE, DEDU1, DEDU2, DEDU3, AGE, $AGE^2$, DURABLA, PRODUCA, DHOUSE, DSEX, DLOC1, DLOC2, DLFS1, DLFS2)

where all variables are the same except FAILURE = 1 if a household is poor and has received no social assistance. If household is poor and has received social assistance FAILURE = 0; for all non-poor households, FAILURE is unobserved; DURABLA = index of ownership of consumer durables is a new RHS variable, while SHRWAGEY is dropped for identification purposes. The rationale is that linkage with the formal labor market (reflected in high value of SHRWAGEY) might explain whether the household is poor or not poor, but not whether it is discriminated in the allocation of social assistance. DURABLA is a composite index of durables ownership. It is obtained by assigning to the ownership of each consumer durable good a value of 1 and then summing up the score (e.g., if a household owns a TV and a refrigerator it would score 2).

Due to the potentially important role that family composition and ownership of durables might have when deciding whether to deliver social assistance (as in means testing), we experiment with different formulations of the regressions. In one set, HHSIZE is replaced by the family composition variables: number of the unemployed in the household (UNEMPLN), number of children (CHILDN) and number of male adults (MADULTN). In the second set, ownership of specific durables—ownership of a car, black and white TV only, refrigerator, personal computer, and so on—are introduced in the equation instead of the composite durables index. This gives a total of four "error of exclusion" equations (2X2 manipulations of the household size/composition and individual durables/index of durables).[33] The equation with household composition (instead of size) and ownership of individual durables, for example, will look like this:

(3)    FAILURE = fct (UNEMPLN, CHILDN, MADULTN, DEDU1, DEDU2, DEDU3, AGE, AGE$^2$, **DCAR, DTV, DPC, DREFRIGERATOR, DMICRO, DSTEREO, DMOTOR,** PRODUCA, DHOUSE, DSEX, DLOC1, DLOC2, LFS1, DLFS2)

where the variables in bold show the ownership of various consumer durables.[34]

Table 3.16 summarizes the results of the error of exclusion regressions with the index of durables (and the two formulations of household, by either size or composition). Table 3.17 summarizes the results of the regressions with individual durables (and, of course, the two formulations of the household variable).

## B.    Non-Discriminant Variables

However before we discuss the variables (shown in Tables 3.16 and 3.17) that are significant in explaining the delivery of social assistance—variables whose presence makes some people *less likely* or *more likely* to be excluded—it is important to focus on the variables whose presence is neutral, which neither help nor disadvantage the poor. Comparing the variables in Tables 3.16 and 3.17 with the variables included in equations (2) and (3), we see that age per se[35] and education of the household head do not matter anywhere except in

**Table 3.16. Explaining error of exclusion: Regressions with the index of durables**

| | Poland | | Bulgaria | | Hungary | | Estonia | | Russia | |
|---|---|---|---|---|---|---|---|---|---|---|
| **Poor who are "discriminated" in favor** | Large households<br>Primary school*<br>Tenancy<br>Female HH<br>Unemployed HH<br>Pensioner HH | No. of unemployed<br>No. of children<br>No. of male adults<br>Primary school<br>Secondary general<br>Female HH*<br>Unemployed HH<br>Pensioner HH | None | None | Other cities<br>Rural areas*<br>Female HH* | No. of children*<br>Other cities<br>Rural areas*<br>Female HH* | Unemployed HH* | | Tenancy*<br>Female HH*<br>Pensioner HH | Tenancy*<br>Pensioner HH |
| **Poor who are "discriminated" against** | Durables<br>Age (squared) | Durables<br>Age (squared)<br>Vocational educ.<br>Production assets<br>Other cities* | None | None | | | Tenancy* | Tenancy* | Other cities<br>Rural areas | Other cities<br>Rural areas |
| **λ significant** | yes, negative | yes, negative | n.a. | n.a. | yes, positive | yes, positive | yes, *<br>positive | no | yes, *<br>positive | yes, *<br>positive |

*Note:* The first column under each country gives the results for the regression using household size as explanatory variable; the second column gives the results using household composition. HH = household head. All coefficients significant at 1% level unless otherwise* noted (5% level).

**Table 3.17.  Explaining error of exclusion: Regressions with individual durables**

| | Poland | | Bulgaria | | Hungary | | Estonia | | Russia | |
|---|---|---|---|---|---|---|---|---|---|---|
| **Poor who are "discriminated" in favor** | Large households, Primary education, Secondary general, Tenancy, Female HH, Pensioner HH | | None | | Other cities, Rural areas*, Female HH*, Unemployed HH, Refrigerator | No. of children*, Other cities, Rural areas*, Female HH, Unemployed HH*, Refrigerator* | Age (squared)* | | Tenancy*, Female HH*, Pensioner HH, Color TV, B/W TV only* | Tenancy*, Female HH*, Pensioner HH, Color TV, B/W TV only* |
| **Poor who are "discriminated" against** | Vocational education, Car, Color TV, Refrigerator, Age (squared), Production assets | | None | Refrigerator | | | Tenancy*, Age | Tenancy* | Other cities, Rural areas | Other cities, Rural areas |
| **λ significant** | yes, negative | | n.a. | n.a. | yes, positive | no | | no | yes, * positive | no |

*Note:* The first column under each country gives the results for the regression using household size as explanatory variable; the second column gives the results using household composition. HH = household head. All coefficients significant at 1% level unless otherwise noted* (5% level).

Poland. This is an important finding because both might have been expected to have a role. For example, people of older age—income and everything else being the same—might be expected to receive a more sympathetic hearing from the social assistance offices than people of working age. There is no evidence for this except for very weak evidence in Poland where very old people seem somewhat discriminated against, and in Estonia, where in one formulation (household size with individual durables; see Table 3.17) there is an inverted U-shaped curve with the highest likelihood of rejection for the working-age household heads. However, since in several countries, as we shall find out below, pensioner household heads are indeed given a preference in distribution of social assistance, the (indirect) effect of age of the household head may still be present.

One might have also expected that the better educated among the poor might have more access to social assistance, because they are likely to be better informed. There is no evidence for that either. Education does not seem to be a factor, with the solitary exception of Poland, where the less educated are shown some preference.

Similarly unimportant is the ownership of production assets (again, with the exception of Poland). This is also a somewhat unexpected result because one could argue that households that have some productive assets should be more easily excluded from assistance on the grounds that they can help themselves. The percentage of such households is not negligible among the poor. (As households with productive assets are considered all households that report some self-employment income.) This percentage varies between 4 and 7 percent for all countries except Estonia, where 28 percent of the poor report self-employment income.

Finally, household size does not play a role anywhere except in Poland, where large families are more likely to be helped.

We now turn to the analysis of the variables that *do* have an impact on the likelihood of receiving social assistance. The set of variables (Tables 3.16 and 3.17) under the title "poor who are 'discriminated' in favor" shows the characteristics that make a given poor household more likely to receive social assistance than another poor household identical in all respects but that one. The second set of characteristics—"poor who are 'discriminated' against"—shows the variables whose presence reduces the likelihood of a *poor* household receiving social assistance.

## C.  The Role of Labor Force Status of the Household Head, and Household Composition

A household headed by an unemployed person will be favored in Poland, Hungary, and Estonia. A household headed by a pensioner will receive more favorable treatment in Poland and Russia. Finally, a female-headed household will be more likely helped than an identical male-headed household in Poland, Hungary, and Russia.

Household composition plays an important role in Poland, and somewhat less so in Hungary. In Poland, the number of the unemployed, children, or male adults in a household are all positively associated with the likelihood of receiving assistance. In Hungary, only the number of children seems to matter. Overall, other than in Bulgaria and, to a lesser extent in Estonia, household composition and headship seem to be taken seriously by social workers when deciding whom to help.

## D.  The Role of Tenancy

Households that are renting their apartments from private individuals, state, or enterprises where they work (as opposed to being owners) seem to be shown preference by social assistance offices in Russia and Poland. This is indeed what we would expect since presumably such households have to bear higher rent costs than owners. However, very puzzlingly, in Estonia the reverse is true: such households are more likely to be *refused* aid. In Hungary and Bulgaria, the tenancy variable has no discernible effect.

## E.  The Role of Location

Location is one of the most interesting variables to study since the often a priori expectation is that one might find some (positive or negative) discrimination based on location. For example, villages may either not receive sufficient funds from the central authorities, or peasants may not know about social assistance, or ascertaining incomes (income testing) may be more difficult in rural areas, thus leading to undersupply of assistance. Estonia, Poland, and Bulgaria show no effect of location on delivery of social assistance. The absence of a locational effect is particularly striking in Poland because almost all other variables do, in one or another formulation, have some impact on the likelihood of exclusion. But location, "stubbornly," does not. However, in Hungary and Russia locational variables do matter. In Hungary, cities other than Budapest and rural areas are treated better than the capital. The effect is very strong, and persists through all four formulations of our regression. In Russia, quite to the contrary, other cities and rural areas are, equally strongly (in all formulations) found to be discriminated against compared to Moscow and St. Petersburg.[36] Thus, in Russia, Moscow, and St. Petersburg seem to enjoy a privileged status; in Hungary, Budapest is discriminated against.

## F.   *The Role of Durables*

We have included durables to check if in lieu of income testing, which is often difficult, the authorities resort to means testing, disqualifying, for example, households that own certain expensive consumer durables like a car or personal computer. The results for Poland are again quite different from those for other countries. In Poland, the composite index of durables as well as ownership of individual durables (car, color TV, refrigerator) are taken by social assistance workers as indicators of a household's better economic position (than other elements would indicate) and such households are more likely to be refused aid. Means testing seems to function in Poland. The results for other countries are far less clear. The composite index of durables is nowhere significant. In Hungary and Bulgaria, ownership of a refrigerator—sole among all durables—seems to matter. But it matters in opposite ways: in Bulgaria (as in Poland) it appears to be considered a luxury (for the poor);[37] in Hungary, it appears to be viewed as an inferior good—even for the poor, ownership of a refrigerator is associated with a greater likelihood of receiving social assistance. It is unclear why a refrigerator is the only of all durables to be considered an inferior good. In Russia, the results for TV ownership are contradictory: both color TV and black and white TV were apparently considered inferior goods (again, alone among all durable goods).[38] In Estonia, ownership of durables does not matter.

## G.    Do Errors of Exclusion Decrease with Decline in Welfare?

One would have expected that errors of exclusion ("deserving" households who do not get aid) would decrease as the objective conditions of households become worse. In other words, it would matter more—for the effectiveness of social assistance—if truly very poor households are excluded than if households who are just below the poverty threshold are excluded. If that were the case, the increase in probability of being poor (the increase of the probit value DPOOR in equation 1) should reduce the likelihood of exclusion in equation 2 or 3. Then the $\lambda$ coefficient (the Mills ratio) would be negative. Only in Poland is $\lambda$ negative and significantly different from zero (at less than 1 percent level). In Russia and Hungary there is, respectively, weak and strong evidence[39] that the error of exclusion *increases* with decline in welfare. In Hungary and Russia, the social assistance system is focused more on those closer to the poverty threshold than on the *very poor*.

## H.    What Can We Conclude about Different Social Assistance Systems?

Similarly to the classification attempted in Section 3.2 we can try to look at the salient differences between the way the social assistance systems operate in different countries. Poland shows by far the greatest importance of various household features in the allocation of social assistance. Most of the "bias" implied by them accords with what we expect: large and tenant households as well as those headed by pensioners, females, and the unemployed are treated more favorably. Households that own consumer durables and production assets are more likely to be refused aid. The reliance on household characteristics and means testing confirms what we would expect from the Polish *Social Assistance Law,* which stipulates that low income is a necessary but not sufficient condition to receive welfare: the presence of other characteristics is often required. The Polish results thus imply that social assistance workers use a large amount of discretion in choosing among the prospective recipients. An absence of the territorial element hints at the relatively centralized nature of social assistance, both in observance of the criteria and funding.

At the other extreme are Bulgarian and Estonian systems where household features have very little to do with the likelihood of rejection. To some extent it may be due to the much smaller sample size in the two countries where a very low eligibility threshold means that relatively few households can qualify (only 2.1 percent in Bulgaria and 2.8 percent in Estonia). Differently, one could argue that their social assistance systems are either dominated by a very strict adherence to income (welfare) testing or that they are fairly random in whom they help. Under both scenarios, the household characteristics would not matter. Since Estonia's system is well targeted, the second possibility (random allocation of social assistance) is not very likely.

The Hungarian and Russian systems lie somewhere in the middle. They concentrate on a few important household characteristics. In Hungary, the households headed by the unemployed are treated better than others;[40] in Russia, households headed by pensioners are treated better. This in turn may owe to the difference in the underlying political economy. In Hungary, regular pensions have preserved the relative position of pensioners much better than in Russia. From the point of view of social workers, pensioners in Russia are therefore much more of a vulnerable category than in Hungary. In Hungary, cities other than Budapest and rural areas have easier access to social assistance; in Russia, the very reverse is the case: other cities and rural areas are discriminated against. A very decentralized nature of social assistance in the two countries (in Hungary, the funding and administration of many social assis-

**Table 3.18.    An attempted classification of the social assistance systems**

| Unified system with strong discretion | Decentralized systems | Strongly income-based or random systems |
|---|---|---|
| Poland | Hungary | Estonia |
| . | Russia | Bulgaria |

tance programs are entirely under county jurisdiction; and social assistance in Russia is notoriously localized) may explain these features of the system.

This leads us to a classification of the systems shown in Table 3.18.

Now, this classification is fairly similar to the classification in Table 3.14, based on the aggregate system characteristics. There as here, Hungary and Russia were classified together even if in terms of their efficiency they differ sharply. The decentralized systems seem to imply large coverage (many people receive benefits) but small amounts of benefits (relative to recipients' income or expenditures). Despite this Hungary has been able to achieve a good focus on the poor and a good pro-poor distribution. This outcome, at the aggregate (country-wide level) is compatible with a decentralized social assistance *only* if the equally poor in various regions of the country are treated approximately the same. This, in turn, implies that social assistance availability (funding) is broadly correlated with local needs, and that the efficiency of funds' distribution is approximately the same across regions. On the contrary, in Russia the decentralized system has resulted in a weak focus on the poor. This most likely occurred because local and regional financial conditions of social assistance offices differ to such a great extent that the same people (in terms of income) are treated very differently in different regions. This then results in a very weak country-wide focus on the poor (since many poor live in poor regions that do not have sufficient funds). The conclusion is that decentralized financing systems seem to produce reasonably good results in a country where territorial differences in income are small. In a country where territorial income differences are large, a decentralized system leads to large horizontal inequities (the same individuals treated differently).

## 3.4. CONCLUSIONS

This chapter had three objectives, addressed in its three sections. In the first section, we looked at the characteristics of social assistance in five transition countries (How many people receive it? How high is the poverty line? How large are disbursements compared to population expenditures?) and its performance (Do the poor have a higher probability of receiving social assistance? Do disbursements decline fast with higher income or welfare levels?). The first section not only provides the background for our next section, and our objective, namely to find out if there is a relationship between the characteristics of social assistance systems and a system's performance, but also offers one of the few analytical and empirical assessments of the countries' welfare systems. Finally, in the third section, the objective was to try to find out if there are specific household characteristics (e.g., living in rural areas, being a single parent) that make poor households less or more likely to receive social assistance.

We can make three types of conclusions. First, regarding what types of social assistance regimes exist in Eastern Europe; second, regarding the link between the type of social assistance regime and its efficiency; and third, regarding the households that are more likely to be excluded from social assistance even if their low welfare level should make them eligible.

By combining the number of recipients of social assistance (relatively few or many) and the amount of social assistance disbursed per recipient household, we obtain a four-way classification where social assistance can be either: (1) *concentrated* (relatively large amounts dispersed to a few households), (2) *dispersed* (relatively small amounts dispersed to many), (3) *irrelevant* (relatively small amounts paid out to a few), or (4) *very important* (relatively large amounts paid out to many). No country belongs to the last group, which is understandable since social assistance (unlike, say, pensions) is supposed to be a social transfer of last resort and is unlikely to be an important source of income for *many* households. Only Bulgaria belongs to the category of irrelevant social assistance. Poland and Estonia have concentrated social assistance regimes: less than 4 percent of the population receives social assistance,[41] but on average social assistance pays for 15 percent (Estonia) to 20 percent (Poland) of recipient households' expenditures. Russia and Hungary have dispersed systems. Almost a quarter of the population in Hungary and 13 percent in Russia receive some form of social assistance. But on average social assistance covers less than 5 percent of recipients' expenditures.

Can these and some other features of social assistance (e.g., if the eligibility threshold is pitched high or low relative to average level of welfare) be related to the targeting efficiency of social assistance? The answer is no. If we measure targeting efficiency by the amount of social assistance that goes to the bottom decile, Estonia and Hungary score very well; Russia, Poland, and Bulgaria score poorly. Indeed, our sample of five countries is too small to be able to claim that such a relationship does not exist. But at least in our sample of transition economies (which account for more than one-half of the population living in transition countries), we were unable to detect this relationship—even if on an a priori basis one might have expected that the concentrated systems might be better targeted. But if in Poland relatively few households receive relatively substantial social assistance, it does not (and in this case, it did not) follow that most of the households that receive such assistance are among the poorest. We are thus left looking for alternative explanations for the varying performance in targeting. Hungary and Russia, despite the fact that they both have dispersed regimes, locally decentralized both in terms of delivery and financing, differ in targeting efficiency. We believe that this is due to the operation of a similar system in vastly different environments. Hungary is a small country without significant regional variations in income; Russia is a vast country with huge regional differences. A system that is almost entirely (Russia) or about half (Hungary) locally financed with, in both cases, broad local discretion in delivery of social assistance, will tend to be dispersed because almost all local authorities will pay some social assistance although the amounts will be small. The system will be badly targeted in a country like Russia, because poorer regions will have less money to disburse to "their" poor (who also would tend to be very poor if country-wide standards are applied), and their administration capacities would tend to be weaker. In Hungary, more homogeneous regional incomes combined with a larger (than in Russia) share of central resources that are distributed in function of local needs, would ensure better targeting.

If one is concerned with poverty alleviation, an important issue is "error of exclusion." It pertains to households that in terms of welfare or income should qualify for social assistance but are either refused the assistance or never claim it. Can we identify some factors that seem to be systematically related to certain types of households being left out of social assistance ("discriminated against") and others being included ("discriminated in favor") more than their income alone would warrant? We find that (other than in Poland) neither age of household head (alone), his or her education level, household's ownership of productive assets, or household size are systematically related to the error of exclusion. This was somewhat of a surprise because we could have expected that older people or larger families or more educated people might either be given more sympathetic hearing or might be better informed about the existence of social assistance. But none of these elements seemed to matter. What did matter was the labor force status of the household head, household composition, and location. In Poland, Hungary, and Estonia a household headed by an unemployed person was "discriminated in favor." So were female-headed households in Poland, Hungary, and Russia, and pensioner-headed households in Poland and Russia. These all seem to be the "correct" types of (positive) discrimination because all three types of households (headed by the unemployed, pensioner, or a female) may be considered to display some handicaps, as for example, inability to increase its labor supply,[42] that might qualify them more for aid than households with a similar level of income but a different composition.

Location was an important variable only in Hungary and Russia. This is, for the reasons mentioned above, related to the heavy regionalization of the systems. In Russia, the system is biased in favor of those who live in the two capitals (Moscow and St. Petersburg) which, by nation-wide standards, are rich regions.[43] This outcome is explicable by greater amounts of assistance available in the capitals, greater visibility of the poor (and hence probably greater awareness both among the poor and the population at large that they should be helped). In the remote areas of Russia, neither funds, nor ability to help, nor maybe the awareness among the poor that they should receive something, may exist. Thus they are left to fend out for themselves.

Ownership of durable goods is often used by social assistance offices in many countries to judge households' welfare (in lieu or in addition to trying to assess income). In our sample, we find the evidence for that only in Poland. In all other countries, ownership of durables either does not matter, or matters in some specific instances in rather unclear or counterintuitive ways (e.g., ownership of refrigerator seems to be viewed as a luxury for the poor in Bulgaria but as an inferior good in Hungary).

Similarly to the classification of social assistance regimes based on their coverage and importance to the recipients, we have tried to classify the regimes according to their treatment of the various categories of the poor ("error of exclusion"). Hungary and Russia, where regional elements are important, belong to the decentralized systems. Poland, on the other hand, is the only country where many of the household characteristics matter in the allocation of social assistance; even officially, eligibility for social assistance depends on the presence of certain household characteristics (so-called "dysfunctionalities"). This, in addition to the absence of regional elements in the error of exclusion, makes us classify Poland as having a centralized system with strong discretion—a system where household characteristics other than income are often used to decide whether to give aid. The Estonian and Bulgarian systems show no evidence of much use of household characteristics. This may be because only a very small number of people qualify as poor in the two countries, which makes it difficult to draw statistically valid conclusions, or because of very strong income testing where household characteristics *per se* are immaterial, or because of the random nature of the allocation of social assistance.

*  *  *

What are the policy implications of our findings? First, if better targeting of social assistance is an important objective, then different types of systems may be appropriate for different countries. A country with large regional differences is unlikely to achieve good targeting if social assistance is mostly locally funded and there is a very broad local discretion in its allocation. (And large regional differences are not confined to territorially large countries: such small countries as Latvia or Serbia have very pronounced regional inequality.) But the same decentralized system may perform better in a different, more homogeneous setting.

Second, strongly regionalized systems such as the Hungarian or Russian display the tendency to exclude from access to social assistance households living in "wrong" regions. This "negative" discrimination seems much more pernicious than the "discrimination in favor" that we find to apply in almost all countries to households headed by the unemployed, females, or pensioners. But the importance given to these three categorical elements implies that income testing alone is nowhere sufficient: social workers obviously feel that the categorical differences are important, and they use them when deciding whom to help.

The policy conclusions are thus:

- Decentralized systems (in terms both of funding and discretion) are not appropriate for countries with large regional income disparities; and even if the disparities are absent, the systems might lead to differences in regional access to social assistance that are difficult to justify (thus violating horizontal equity).
- Income testing alone is not sufficient. It needs to be combined with the use of categorical criteria.
- The combination of categorical and income testing should be, in most cases, implemented within a relatively centralized system where people's access to social assistance does not depend on location.

CHAPTER 4

# POLICY RECOMMENDATIONS AND GENERAL CONCLUSIONS

JEANINE BRAITHWAITE, CHRISTIAAN
GROOTAERT, AND BRANKO MILANOVIC

This book reported the results of two analytic tasks: the construction of a comparative poverty profile for six countries of Eastern Europe and the former Soviet Union, and an assessment of the social assistance delivery systems in these countries. To that effect, we constructed a comparative data set, whereby household survey data from the six countries (Bulgaria, Hungary, Poland, Estonia, Kyrgyz republic, and Russia) were carefully checked, cleaned, and made comparable. We dubbed this data set HEIDE—Household Expenditure and Income Data for Transitional Economies.

The most striking finding is how different the post-Soviet experience with poverty and targeting is from the East European one. Overcoming the Soviet legacy has not been as easy as the generally positive East European transitions would have suggested. FSU governments face a double challenge: poverty levels are higher than in Eastern

Europe, but poverty correlates are not as sharp or as well-defined. Both factors will make it harder to reduce poverty and to target assistance.

## A.   *Incidence of Poverty*

In contrast to preceding periods, there was a sharp increase in poverty in both Eastern Europe and the former Soviet Union (FSU) during the transition to a market economy. In Eastern Europe, the start of the rapid transition in the early 1990s accelerated the existing trend toward increasing poverty, mainly as a result of the loss of employment in a suddenly contracting state sector without coincident emergence of private sector employment. In the FSU, large increases in measured poverty reflect the impact of severe macroeconomic problems, including collapse in GDP and hyperinflation, sharp increases in income inequality, and measurement error that understated poverty before transition.

We found that poverty rates as well as poverty gaps are lower in Eastern Europe than the FSU. In the period of this study (1993–1995), FSU poverty rates exceeded 30 percent, and the poverty gaps exceeded 20 percent, with the worst cases being Russia (poverty rate of almost 40 percent and average poverty gap of 30 percent) and the Kyrgyz republic (poverty incidence of 43 percent). The lowest poverty rates were those in Hungary (21 percent) and Poland (23 percent). Bulgaria and Estonia were intermediate between these two extremes.

Based on the average poverty gaps, poverty is shallower in Eastern Europe, suggesting that as economic growth strengthens, rising incomes may pull many people above the poverty line. Deeper poverty in the FSU makes this unlikely, and suggests that the poverty problem is more likely to persist there. Poverty in Eastern Europe has become more like poverty in Western Europe—highly correlated with individual skills and labor market possibilities—while in the FSU poverty is more pervasive and ill-defined.

## B.   *Poverty Profile*

The profile of poverty was generally sharper in Eastern Europe than in the former Soviet Union, meaning that there are more differences between poverty rates and gaps of the various groups considered. This reflects the differences in adjustment to the introduction of the market economy between the two regions.

In all six countries, location played a major role, with the dominating effect stemming from living in the capital. Poverty incidence in the capital cities was anywhere from 9 to 21 percentage points lower than the national poverty rate. In Poland and Russia, poverty rates in the capital city were even less than half the national rates. The only exception to this pattern was Hungary, where the capital city has a higher poverty incidence than other cities. In all six countries, rural poverty rates were sharply higher than urban rates.

Family composition and household size are strongly correlated with poverty in the six transition economies studied. In Eastern Europe and Russia, the poverty rates of households with three or more children are approximately double the average, but even in the Kyrgyz republic and Estonia the rate is well above the average. The strong implication is that poverty among children is higher than average throughout the six countries. This finding constitutes a call to reform entitlement programs, such as family allowances that provide fixed amounts of money to households with children. Clearly, throughout Eastern Europe and the FSU, these programs are insufficient to prevent households with many children from falling into poverty. A possible solution is to introduce means testing or proxy means testing in order to eliminate the allowances for rich households and to increase the amounts given to large poor households.

Apart from large households, poverty incidence and gaps are also higher in households consisting of only one adult in all of the countries except Poland (where the pension system is exceptionally generous). Most of these households are pensioners and the majority are women. Poverty rates for elderly women are higher than for elderly men.

In Eastern Europe, open unemployment emerged along with real wage declines, but in the FSU, much of the adjustment fell exclusively on real wages. Despite real wage declines, in all six countries, wage earners and the self-employed had the lowest poverty rates and gaps among different socioeconomic categories. Open unemployment among household members sharply increased the risk of poverty in four of the countries. In the case of FSU, a special problem is created by the pervasive arrears in payment of wages and pensions, which increases transitory poverty.

In Eastern Europe, the link between lower poverty and higher education is quite pronounced, but the link is much weaker in the FSU (and practically non-existent in the Kyrgyz republic). This reflects the stage of transition, whereby as transition advances, the emerging private sector requires well-educated workers with flexible and adaptable general education backgrounds. Low-skill jobs held by workers with primary education or less have disappeared in great numbers in Eastern Europe. In the FSU, where the transition is not as advanced, higher education still means less chance of poverty for the household, but not to the same extent as in Eastern Europe.

Female-headed households have much higher poverty rates than male-headed ones in all countries except Poland, where this difference is small. Poverty gaps for female-headed households are much higher in the FSU than in Eastern Europe. For many women, the labor market changes of transition have had major implications. Prior to transition, women were expected to work full time but the state provided day care for their children. Transition has led to a drop in female labor force participation as well as to a reduced supply of affordable day care centers. Both factors are likely to affect female-headed households disproportionately. Information on age suggests that poverty rates decrease during the active-age years, but sharply increase after age 65. Since the majority of those living past 65 are women, gender is a relevant poverty dimension in Eastern Europe and the FSU.

## C.  Multivariate Analysis of Welfare and Poverty

Our objective was to assess the relative importance of the various correlates of poverty and if possible, to attribute causality. Since determinants of welfare such as the demographic profile of households or the returns to assets may vary between the poor and non-poor, the multivariate analysis would help to clarify these differences. There was a marked difference in the findings between

Eastern Europe (where most variables were significant, indicating a consistent set of factors significant for welfare outcomes) and the FSU (where the explanatory power of the welfare regressions was low and fewer variables were found to be significant).

In Eastern Europe, the general pattern of findings is that education and the ownership of a household enterprise have the largest effects on welfare outcomes, followed by the nature of the household's link with the labor market. Demographic characteristics are a distant third. These results underscore the crucial importance of general education (especially post-secondary education) for a successful long-term strategy of coping with transition. The regression results point at huge gaps in the returns to education between the primary and higher education levels, which is a major factor behind the increases in inequality in the distribution of welfare following transition.

In the FSU, locational factors have the strongest effect on household welfare, followed by the share of wages in household income, whether or not the household has a household enterprise, and higher education. The locational disparities in welfare are so large as to be unlikely to be rectified even in the medium to long term. Hence, the policy emphasis will have to fall on improving the functioning of the labor market, especially its ability to create jobs and pay workers on time. The importance of entrepreneurial activity for increasing household welfare should not be overlooked. Microcredit programs and small-business incubators in Russia have shown promising results.

We considered the possibility that measurement error in the household expenditure data could be correlated with some of the explanatory variables in the model, and we also estimated poverty probit models to check for consistency in results. Poverty models are less sensitive to such correlations and may also overcome problems stemming from a low statistical fit of the specific functional form (e.g., linear or log-linear) of the welfare regression on the actual distribution. In general, for both the East European countries and the FSU, the probit results were consistent with the findings of the welfare regressions. However, there were some quantitative differences in the relative importance of a given factor, reflecting the fact that the poverty regression uses different information than the welfare regression.

Quantile regressions estimating the regression line through given points on the distribution of the dependent variable were calculated at the tenth, twenty-fifth, fiftieth, seventy-fifth, and ninetieth percentiles. In Eastern Europe, education was generally more significant below the median, while enterprise ownership was typically more important above the median. The effect of unemployment was different across the countries, strongest below the median in Hungary, above the median in Poland.

Interestingly, in Russia and the Kyrgyz republic, returns to university education fall dramatically as one moves up the distribution, to the point of becoming insignificant at the ninetieth percentile. This clearly indicates that factors other than education explain high incomes in these countries, including factors not captured in the model. We discussed earlier the role of the share of wages and the ownership of a household enterprise as determinants of welfare. The quantile regressions showed that these factors matter most for households at or below the median. Creating wage jobs and facilitating the creation of household enterprises hence need to be cornerstones in labor market policies and poverty alleviation efforts in the FSU. Lastly, unlike in Eastern Europe, land ownership is as important or more important than other assets in the FSU.

We found some noteworthy interactions between education level and entrepreneurial behavior, based on regressions on subsamples split by education level of the head of household. For example, in Bulgaria, the return to owning a household enterprise is almost double for a head of household with higher education, but in Poland, the highest returns are for household enterprises owned by heads of household with only primary education. The results are even more differentiated for the FSU, where returns to owning an enterprise are highest for heads of household with primary education in Estonia, for those with vocational education in the Kyrgyz republic, and for those with secondary education in Russia. Several factors interact to explain these results: the stage of transition, the prevailing type of enterprises, and the distribution of education.

## D.  Indicator-Based Targeting

Indicator-based targeting of social assistance payments is useful in country contexts where overall means testing is prohibitively costly, difficult to administer, or where income declarations are highly unreliable. This characterizes Eastern Europe to a certain extent, and is especially the case in the FSU. We tried to answer the question of whether indicator-based targeting would be effective in identifying the poor, using as the indicators the same set of variables examined in the welfare and poverty regressions. We compared the predicted values to the actual values of the dependent variable, using an expanded welfare regression with additional predictors, and calculated the percentage of correct predictions.

In general, we found that the models did a much better job of identifying the non-poor than the poor, and that overall identification rates were much better in Eastern Europe than in the FSU. This is in line, of course, with the better statistical fit of the welfare models in Eastern Europe, as discussed earlier.

We attempted to improve upon the predictive ability of the indicators by designing a two-stage process. We assumed that it would be possible in a first stage to screen out the upper half of the distribution. For Eastern Europe, this assumption proved reasonable since we could correctly identify, with the same set of indicators, close to 90 percent of the non-poor in Bulgaria and close to 100 percent of the non-poor in Hungary and Poland. However, in the FSU, the identification rates for the non-poor were lower, around 70 percent.

The second stage of the simulation demonstrated that for Eastern Europe, the indicator-targeting approach was able to correctly identify the poor—about 60 percent of the poor in Poland and nearly 90 percent in Bulgaria (Table 4.1). In Hungary and Bulgaria, using only the five best predictors achieved an identification rate virtually on a par with the full model. In the FSU, the two-stage simulation led to a correct identification of 65 percent of the poor in Estonia and 80 percent of the poor in Russia and the Kyrgyz republic. On the other hand, in two of the three FSU countries (Russia and the Kyrgyz republic), the identification of the non-poor in the second

**Table 4.1.   Percent correct predictions (two-stage process)**

|          | Bulgaria | Hungary | Poland | Estonia | Kyrgyz republic | Russia |
|----------|----------|---------|--------|---------|-----------------|--------|
| Poor     | 86.7     | 67.8    | 60.4   | 65.5    | 83.1            | 79.5   |
| Non-poor | 35.9     | 70.9    | 75.0   | 61.1    | 8.7             | 21.8   |
| All      | 63.9     | 69.7    | 69.5   | 65.1    | 81.3            | 72.9   |

stage was particularly bad, suggesting that in the FSU, the two-stage method is more prone to inclusion error (giving assistance to non-poor) than to exclusion error (denying assistance to the poor).

The results of these simulations suggest that fairly simple indicator-based targeting methods are capable of levels of correct identification of the poor that far exceed those of the systems currently in place in the countries (where leakage rates, i.e., benefits going to the non-poor, often exceed 50 percent). The policy implication is that such two-stage indicator-based targeting methods deserve consideration for real-life application. The robustness of such methods is highlighted by the fact that, at least in Eastern Europe, the loss of accuracy was quite small when using the five or ten best predictors. In the FSU, results were less impressive but still better than the existing systems. Already in Russia, pilot experiments have been conducted with indicator targeting in Volgograd oblast as a part of World Bank-supported social policy reforms.

## E.   Efficiency of Social Assistance

Social assistance rather unexpectedly was assigned a major role during the transition from planned to market economy. This happened as incomes tumbled, poverty exploded, and the socialist safety net organized around enterprise-provided protection evaporated. Within a few years after the beginning of the transition many people, maybe as many as 100 million, fell below the poverty line (Milanovic, 1998). But the decline in real incomes that triggered this massive increase in poverty also implied that fewer resources were available for the governments to redress poverty through social assistance—a transfer of last resort. Thus, the attention shifted on how the meager

**Table 4.2.    Leakage of social assistance (in percent)
(using national definitions of poverty)**

|          | Leakage in terms of recipients | Leakage in terms of amounts of funds |
|----------|:------------------------------:|:------------------------------------:|
| Poland   | 35.5 | 34.3 |
| Hungary  | 86.7 | 77.1 |
| Bulgaria | 92.0 | 88.1 |
| Estonia  | 84.1 | 88.1 |
| Russia   | 64.6 | 64.0 |

*Note*: Leakage is defined as percent of all recipients and all money that is not disbursed to the poor (according to the national definition of poverty).

funds that are available might be used to help the most needy. The concern with improvement in the efficiency of social assistance was born out of this double development: increasing needs on the one side, and shrinking means on the other.

Our objective was to assess the efficiency of current social assistance systems in five HEIDE countries (Poland, Hungary, Bulgaria, Estonia, and Russia), using the countries' own poverty lines (i.e., eligibility thresholds for social assistance). Consider Table 4.2, which gives the percentage of leakage in terms of people (the non-poor who receive social assistance) and in terms of money (the amount of money that is paid out to the non-poor). Leakage seems to be huge. The percentage of money that goes to the non-poor ranges, with the exception of Poland, between 64 and 88 percent. For each unit of local currency disbursed to a poor person (poor according to the country's own definition), social assistance systems disburse up to 7 units to the non-poor. Or in other words, in order to deliver $1 to a poor, the social assistance costs range between $1.50 and $8 (excluding the administrative costs of delivery).

While these results are useful in alerting us to the amounts that are not best used, given the countries' own definitions of who is—at least in monetary (income) terms—eligible for social assistance, they are not useful for comparing the performances of various social assistance systems and drawing some general lessons. This is because the results displayed in Table 4.2 are also the product of how low or high is the eligibility threshold pitched in each country, and—a more difficult thing to take into account—how other categorical criteria (long-standing illness, presence of handicapped persons in the family, etc.) interplay with the income test in determining who receives social assistance and who is refused. For example, if the eligibility threshold is high, many people will qualify for social assistance. This is the case of Poland where almost 38 percent of households are eligible. Very likely, then, the leakage will be relatively small because not much assistance will be paid to the better-off, who are practically the only non-eligible section of the population. But the reverse situation will occur when the eligibility threshold is very low, as for example in Estonia and Bulgaria, where less than 3 percent of households are eligible for assistance. It is unlikely there that social assistance offices would be able to target their funds so well, and on so few people, that the leakage is small. The extent of leakage shown in Table 4.2 is—everything else being the same—inversely related to the relative level of the poverty line.

In order to eliminate this effect, and thus try to derive some policy conclusions from the ways that different social assistance systems operate and perform, we consider the efficiency of the social assistance in reaching the bottom decile (the poorest 10 percent of the population) in each country. First, we try to classify the social assistance systems in the five countries. By combining the number of recipients of social assistance (relatively few or many) and the amount of social assistance disbursed per recipient household, we obtain a four-way classification where social assistance could be either: (1) *concentrated* (relatively large amounts dispersed to a few households), (2) *dispersed* (relatively small amounts dispersed to many), (3) *irrelevant* (relatively small amounts paid out to a few), or (4) *very important* (relatively large amounts paid out to many). Understandably, no HEIDE country belongs to the last group. Bulgaria belongs to the category of irrelevant social assistance. Poland and Estonia have concentrated social assistance regimes: under 4 percent of the population receives social assistance, but on average social assistance pays for 15 (Estonia) or 20 (Poland) percent of recipient expenditures. Russia and Hungary have dispersed systems. Almost a quarter of the population in Hungary and 13 percent in

**Table 4.3.    Leakage of social assistance (in percent)**
**(poor = bottom decile according to per capita**
**expenditure)**

|  | Leakage in terms of recipients | Leakage in terms of amounts of funds |
|---|---|---|
| Poland | 79.4 | 79.5 |
| Hungary | 83.7 | 72.8 |
| Bulgaria | 82.5 | 77.7 |
| Estonia | 78.3 | 65.3 |
| Russia | 91.3 | 91.8 |

*Note*: Leakage is defined as percent of all recipients and all money that is not disbursed to the poor (where poor are defined as the poorest decile of the population according to household per capita expenditures).

Russia receive some form of social assistance. But on average social assistance covers less than 5 percent of recipients' expenditures.

The next step is to try to associate the typology with targeting efficiency. Now, we measure efficiency by the percentage of social assistance that goes to the bottom decile. (The efficiency is obtained as 100 *minus* the values in Table 4.3). Estonia and Hungary score reasonably well (respectively, 34.7 and 27.2 percent is disbursed to the bottom decile), Poland and Bulgaria score about average (20.5 and 22.3 percent, respectively), and Russia does poorly (8.2 percent). While our sample of five countries is too small to claim whether such a relationship exists in general, at least in our HEIDE sample of transition economies (which accounts for more than one-half of the population living in transition countries in Europe), we were unable to uncover a relationship between the type of social assistance system and its efficiency. Estonia and Poland have concentrated systems, but their efficiency is different; Hungary and Russia have dispersed systems, but their efficiency, too, is different.

These results, however, lead us to focus on why Hungary and Russia, which have dispersed regimes, locally decentralized in terms of delivery and financing, have such vastly different performances. A reason may be that the similar dispersed regimes operate in very different environments. Hungary is a small country without significant regional variations in income; Russia is a vast country with huge regional differences. A system that is to a large extent locally financed, with broad local discretion in delivery of social assistance, will tend to fit our category of "dispersed" systems because most local authorities will pay some social assistance, and the amounts will be small. Such a system will be badly targeted in a country like Russia, where differences between the regions are large and where poor regions will have little money to disburse to "their" poor. Thus, the most needy will receive the least. On the other hand, more equal average incomes by region in Hungary will imply that no region will be so poor that it would lack funds to help "its" poor. One of the policy conclusions is, therefore, that the same or similar social assistance systems may be expected to yield very different results if the underlying conditions are different. A centrally funded system with central eligibility guidelines is more appropriate for countries with large regional income variation.

### F.    Why Are Eligible People Refused Social Assistance?

Another important issue is errors of exclusion. Errors of exclusion occur when households that in terms of welfare or income should qualify for social assistance are either refused the assistance or never claim it. We have tried to study factors that are systematically related to errors of exclusion. While efficiency of social assistance analysis allows us to find out how well or badly social assistance operates, errors of exclusion analysis carries this further. By focusing on the factors that explain why some households are "discriminated against" and others "discriminated in favor," we describe the *modus operandi* of the systems, that is, we look at what underlies a given performance.

First, we were expecting that age of household head, or household head's education level, or household size might be negatively related to the errors of exclusion (older or more educated household heads, or large households, are less likely, we thought, to be discriminated against). Yet we do not find evidence that either of these factors matters—except for the household size and age in Poland.

Who was, then, "discriminated in favor"? Table 4.4 shows that

**Table 4.4.  Households who are "discriminated in favor" and where**

| | |
|---|---|
| Household headed by unemployed | Poland, Hungary, Estonia |
| Household headed by female | Poland, Hungary, Russia |
| Household headed by pensioner | Poland, Russia |
| People who do not possess certain durables (car, productive assets) | Poland |
| People in major cities | Russia |
| People in rural areas | Hungary |

in most cases, these were the "right" types of households—or at least those who we would expect would be more favorably treated: households headed by the unemployed, females, or pensioners.

There was, however, also location-based discrimination in Russia and Hungary. This is related to the reasons mentioned before—strong regionalization of the social assistance systems. In Russia, the system is biased in favor of those who live in the two major cities (Moscow and St. Petersburg) which, by nation-wide standards, are rich. In Hungary, it is the reverse: rural areas are favored.

The results show that in Poland household characteristics other than income are often used to decide whether to help a given household. This fact, combined with the absence of regional-based discrimination, allows us to define Poland's system as a centralized system with strong local discretion. While eligibility rules and most of the financing are centralized, Polish social assistance laws allow local social assistance offices to retain significant autonomy in deciding what weight to give to different central eligibility criteria. A glance at Table 4.3 shows that household characteristics are important in Hungary and Russia too, and somewhat less in Estonia.

There are several policy implications in these findings. First, we find again that strongly decentralized systems like the Russian and Hungarian tend to produce region-based discrimination in the allocation of social assistance. Such systems will tend to exclude households living in "wrong" (poor) regions from access to social assistance. This "negative" discrimination is more pernicious—because it applies particularly to the people who should be helped—than the "discrimination in favor" that applies in almost all countries to households headed by the unemployed, females, or pensioners. Second, the fact that we find categorical characteristics to matter for the allocation of social assistance implies that social assistance workers feel, whether or not they are supported in it by their countries' legislations, that income testing alone is not sufficient.

# NOTES

## PREFACE

1. We have thought it nevertheless useful to offer to the researchers, with all the appropriate caveats, the results of the Armenian and Slovak surveys in the same framework as the rest of the data base.
2. There are 13 expenditure variables, 23 income variables, 25 household asset variables, 5 household characteristic variables, and 6 individual characteristic variables.
3. Further information is available at www.worldbank.org/research/transition/index.html

## CHAPTER ONE

1. The average world population density is about 45 persons per square kilometer.
2. Greece's GDP per capita (according to the *International comparison project*) was $PPP 12,700.
3. This is still significantly above the 6–8 rates in Western Europe and North America.
4. In the Kyrgyz republic, food accounts for two-thirds of all expenditures.
5. Housing expenditures in Russia are only 2 percent of all expenditures, while in Bulgaria they are 26 percent. In Hungary, Estonia, and Poland, they are around 15 percent.
6. This is calculated as the distance between the two vectors of expenditure shares. If there are only two goods, the average distance will be: $(1/2)\sqrt{(X_{11}-X_{21}) + (X_{12}-X_{22})}$ where Xij is the share of $j$-th type of expenditures in $i$-th country.
7. Except in the Kyrgyz republic.

# CHAPTER TWO

1. This is only recently the case in East European countries. Prior to transition, income was usually better reported, because most income sources were under the direct control of the state, and data collection agencies could verify reported income at the source. This is why most pre-transition analyses of poverty have used income-based measures. After transition, the emergence of private sector income (especially self-employment income) has led to a decline in reliability of reported income data, in line with the experience of Western countries (see, for example, Revesz, 1994 for the case of Hungarian income and expenditure data).

2. For the household sizes typically found in Eastern Europe and the FSU, this formulation is a close equivalent of the more conventional statement of the OECD scale whereby the first adult=1, other adults=0.7, and children=0.5. The exponential formulation however simplifies the calculations.

3. It is generally agreed that poverty measures should be calculated over individuals. Hence the relative poverty line was defined over an individual distribution, under the assumption that each individual in the household has the same welfare, equal to total household expenditure per equivalent adult.

4. In making this selection, we trade off "ideal-ness" of the poverty measures for the sake of familiarity and ease of interpretation. An ideal poverty measure must meet the monotonicity axiom (all other things equal, a reduction in the income of a poor person must increase the poverty measure) and the transfer axiom (all other things equal, a net transfer of income from a poorer to a richer person must increase the poverty measure). Neither $P_0$ nor $P_1/P_0$ meet these axioms, but their product, $P_1$, meets the monotonicity axiom. In general, the P-alpha class of measures meets the monotonicity axiom for $\alpha > 0$, and the transfer axiom for $\alpha > 1$ (Foster, Greer, and Thorbecke, 1984).

5. Specifically, the coefficients show the effect of a marginal change in an explanatory variable on the xth conditional quantile of the dependent variable (Buchinsky, 1998).

6. To our knowledge, the first use of such model in the empirical poverty literature is by Bardhan (1984) in a study of poverty in rural West Bengal.

7. In an inter-generational context, even parental characteristics can be endogenous.

8. The annex to this chapter shows the means and standard deviations for the full set of variables used in estimating the welfare and poverty equations.

9. It would also be possible to use a step-wise poverty probit equation for this objective. However, most social assistance authorities are interested not just in classifying applicants as poor/non-poor but also in determining the extent of the welfare shortfall. Hence, the OLS welfare equation is a more useful basis for a predictive model.

10. See Milanovic (1990) for an analysis of pre-transition trends in poverty.

11. The pension system in Poland is discussed in detail in World Bank (1993) and Perraudin and Pujol (1994). For a more general discussion of pension systems in transition economies, see World Bank (1994).

12. The effect of transition on women is discussed further by Einhorn (1993), Funk and Mueller (1993), Chase (1995) and Fong (1996).

13. World Bank, 1995 a-c, 1996 a-d.

14. This definition of "children" as under the age of 15 is arbitrary, as are all definitions that do not correspond to the age of legal majority, which in most of the countries in this study was 18. However, children aged 15–18 have significant economic potential, and in the FSU could usually drop out of school around the age of 14 during the period when the surveys were conducted.

15. One can assume that the effect is the most severe if the head of household is unemployed. Grootaert (1997a) contains some evidence to that effect for Hungary. Since the household head was defined as the main earner in the Poland and Hungary household surveys used for the HEIDE database, few heads of household are classified as unemployed for those countries.

16. This result is clearly sensitive to where exactly the poverty line is set.

17. This is possibly due to recording/measurement errors for this variable, which is carried in the data set as hectares of land held by the household. When the raw data were examined, there were several improbable outliers. Unfortunately, removing these outliers did not significantly improve performance, nor did the substitution of a dummy variable for land ownership. The dummy variable did perform better in Russia than the number of hectares, so it was retained. Somewhat similar measurement problems also plagued the Kyrgyz republic data (the two surveys were conducted by the same consulting group), but the dummy variable was significant for Kyrgyz republic. In Estonia, a different survey and

methodology recorded only whether the household had access to land, not the number of hectares.

18. For Estonia, data on household heads with vocational-technical education were combined with households with general secondary education.

19. At the time of this writing, of the FSU countries, only Armenia had instituted a full-scale land privatization program (1992) by which former state and collective farms had been broken up and all land holdings passed to individuals. In the other countries, households retained access to land through their private plots. Under Soviet law, rural and even urban households were entitled to a very small (less than 0.06 and 0.02 hectares, respectively) plot of land. These land plots were passed from generation to generation, constituted 3 percent of arable Soviet land, and produced up to 25 percent of the gross output of (non-wheat) agricultural production (Gregory and Stuart, 1990).

20. For a discussion of indicator-based targeting in other regions, see, for example, Grosh and Baker (1995) for Latin America and Subbarao et al. (1997) for other regions.

21. Note that adding variables only ensures a better overall prediction rate. The accuracy of predictions for the poor or non-poor separately may actually decline. This is the case, for example, for Bulgaria, where the best five predictors correctly identify 87.8 percent of poor households, but the full model identifies only 86.7 percent of poor households correctly. The overall prediction success rate rose from 60.6 percent to 63.9 percent, however.

22. Analysis of individual countries (Russia, Kyrgyz republic) in World Bank poverty assessments and comparative analyses (Krumm, Milanovic, and Walton, 1994) found that in general, only child allowances were well-targeted transfers in FSU countries. All other transfers were regressive or highly regressive.

23. Restricting the observations to those below the median significantly improved identification of the poor in the Kyrgyz republic and Russia but worsened the identification of the non-poor, which thus prompted an additional experiment with other regressors, in an ultimately futile attempt to improve the predictions of household consumption. Adding "kitchen sink" variables like housing amenities (hot water, central heating, etc.) and an additional dummy variable for self-employed household head resulted in error rates that were virtually identical to those for the original specification for Estonia and Kyrgyz republic and were only marginally better (2–3 percent) for Russia. This specification was therefore not further considered.

# CHAPTER THREE

1. See *Act on Social Assistance 1990*, article 3 (reprinted in Institute of Labor and Social Studies, 1994). After the 1992 amendments, local authorities have the right to refuse benefit if "the actual life situation of the applicant does not reflect the submitted income information." This is an important clause that led to the increased use of means testing.

2. The correlation between expenditure-poor (POORX) and income-poor (POORY) was 0.58; the correlation between per capita expenditures and income was 0.68.

3. Social assistance as defined in the Polish *Household Budget Survey* includes income-tested scholarship; social assistance from enterprises; alimony from social fund; social assistance for nursing; and general social assistance. It does not include a housing allowance.

4. The number of households in each percentile (dot) will vary from country to country depending on the overall country sample size.

5. Zl. 0.36 billion divided by zl. 8.8 billion.

6. Expenditure-based (*after* social assistance) poverty gap is zl. 8.8 billion. zl. 0.36 billion was disbursed to the poor. Thus, *before* social assistance, the poverty gap was zl. 9.16 billion (8.8+0.36). Out of it zl. 0.36 billion, or 3.9 percent, was eliminated.

7. When averaging across households, we calculate the average by giving to each household an equal weight. Thus the ratio social assistance (SA) / poverty gap (PG) is calculated for each individual household, and an average of SA/PG ratios is the mean represented here. Differently, if we concentrate on money amounts, the mean is calculated by simply dividing all social assistance disbursed to the poor and total poverty gap.

8. The expected amount to be received is, as we saw, fairly constant.

9. Local governments adopted more than 2,500 local decrees that specify eligibility conditions and benefit levels (see Sipos, 1995, p. 2).

10. For example, income supplement for the long-term unemployed was set at 80 percent of the minimum pension.

11. The correlation between the expenditure- and income-poor is 0.4; the correlation between income per capita and expenditures per capita is 0.6.

12. Note that the *highest* percentile likelihood of receiving social assistance in Poland is about 10 percent.

13. The difference is less on per capita basis, because the poor recipient households are larger (four members per household vs. only 2.7 for the non-poor).

14. Against 23.3 percent in money terms (see Table 3.4).

15. The correlation between the income- and expenditure-poor is only 0.27; the correlation between per capita income and expenditures is similarly low (0.45).

16. To some extent low poverty line is also due to the use of implicit equivalence scales. This is different from Poland and Hungary where poverty lines were defined in per capita terms.

17. This is a household-weighted average.

18. This amount was substantially less than the minimum pension (EEK 482), which, as we have seen, was used as the poverty line in Poland and Hungary.

19. The correlation between expenditure-poor (POORX) and income-poor (POORY) was only 0.28; the correlation between per capita income and expenditures was 0.60.

20. Based on unweighted sample, the percentage of the poor is 3.8; thus the vertical line in Figure 3.13 is drawn at x=4.

21. Social assistance as defined in the Estonian survey does not include a housing benefit because it is paid directly to municipal enterprises (on the basis of income testing; see World Bank, 1996, p. 28). Social assistance includes: subsistence benefit; other types of support from state or local government; and social support from enterprises.

22. This is household-based average. The actual average (amount of social assistance divided by the number of people in the sample) was about EEK 10 or less than $1 per month.

23. For comparison, in Bulgaria, the poor-to-non-poor ratio of probabilities was 4:1; in Poland 3:1, and in Hungary only 1.6:1.

24. The large difference between the 42 percent average based on households and 18 percent average based on money reflects the fact that the very small poverty gaps were "covered" fully or even in excess of 100 percent (see the value for the third percentile in Figure 3.15).

25. All data are expressed in November 1993 Moscow and St. Petersburg prices.

26. See also Klugman, ed. (1997).

27. Note that the correlation between per capita incomes and expenditures is 0.86 in Slovakia; it lies between 0.6 and 0.7 in Poland, Hungary, and Estonia.

28. Social assistance as defined in the *Russian Longitudinal Monitoring Survey* does not include utilities and housing allowance. Included is only the social assistance received from local authorities.

29. The definitions of efficiency and effectiveness are from Beckerman (1979).

30. Effectiveness is defined as SA1/PG1 where SA1=social assistance disbursed to the first decile, PG1=poverty gap of the first decile. Relative effectiveness is equal to (SA1/PG1) divided by (SA/X) where SA=total social assistance and X=total expenditures.

31. The rationale for the use of the efficiency criterion is obvious. As for "relative" effectiveness (effectiveness per unit of spending), it is preferred to effectiveness alone because we want to abstract from the amount of social assistance given, which is not strictly speaking a performance criterion, but rather a characteristic of the system.

32. Since we have a limited dependent variable, OLS estimators would be biased. We thus need to use ML methods. This is an improvement over the usual, and until recently more common, Heckman two-stage estimation, which solved the problem of selection bias but, by not using maximum likelihood estimation, still yielded inefficient (even if consistent) estimates. Until recently, using Heckman correction with ML methods was computationally prohibitive.

33. As the "error of exclusion" equation is modified (e.g., by including household composition instead of size), so is, in order to maintain the conditions for the exact identification, the first equation.

34. Not all the countries will have the same durables included in the equation. It will depend on data availability.

35. That is regardless of whether a person is a pensioner or not.

36. Moscow and St. Petersburg are both considered to be "the capitals" in our locational variable for Russia.

37. This might well be due to the very small sample size of those eligible to receive social assistance in Bulgaria (2 percent of the population) where apparently ownership of a refrigerator was regarded as an indicator of relative wealth. (Interestingly, other durables like car, stereo equipment, color TV do not matter, although this is probably because they are very rare among the poor.)

38. Our expectation was that only the black and white TV would be considered an inferior good. The results did not bear out this hypothesis.

39. The $\lambda$ coefficient is positive and significant at the 5 percent level in Russia and at 1 percent in Hungary.

40. There is a special program of social assistance for the long-term unemployed.

41. Exclusive of housing benefits.

42. A pensioner cannot easily get a job; an unemployed person is, by definition, *trying* but failing to find one; a female household head typically has much greater responsibility for children than a male household head.

43. According to the RLMS Survey (see Chapter 1), Moscow and St. Petersburg had expenditures per capita some 42 percent above the country-wide average. According to the Goskomstat household data for 1994, Moscow's per capita was 3.5 times the country average, and St. Petersburg's was 12 percent above the Russia average (Goskomstat Rossii, 1995, p. 607).

# References

Alderman, H. and M. Garcia. (1993). "Poverty, Household Food Security, and Nutrition in Rural Pakistan." *International Food Policy Research Institute Research Report No. 96.* Washington, DC: International Food Policy Research Institute.

Appleton, S. (1995). "The Rich are Just Like Us, Only Richer—Poverty Functions or Consumption Functions?" *Centre for the Study of African Economies Working Paper No. 95–4.* Oxford: University of Oxford.

Appleton, S. (1996). "Women-headed Households and Household Welfare: An Empirical Deconstruction for Uganda." *World Development* 24 (12): 1811–1827.

Atkinson, A. and J. Micklewright. (1992). *Economic Transformation in Eastern Europe and the Distribution of Income.* Cambridge, UK: Cambridge University Press.

Bardhan, P. K. (1984). *Land, Labor and Rural Poverty.* Delhi: Oxford University Press.

Beckerman, W. (1979). "The Impact of Income Maintenance Payments on Poverty in Britain." *Economic Journal* 86 (June).

Braithwaite, J. (1990). "Income Distribution and Poverty in the Soviet Republics." *Journal of Soviet Nationalities* 1 (3).

Braithwaite, J. (1991). "The Social Safety Net in the Sovereign Republics." Paper presented at the American Association for the Advancement of Slavic Studies National Convention, November.

Braithwaite, J. (1995). "The Old and New Poor in Russia: Trends in Poverty." Education & Social Policy Department Working Paper No. 57. Washington, DC: World Bank.

Buchinsky, M. (1998). "Recent Advances in Quantile Regression Models." *Journal of Human Resources* 33 (1): 88–126.

Chase, R. (1995). "Women's Labor Force Participation During and After Communism: A Case Study of the Czech Republic and Slovakia." Economic Growth Center Discussion Paper No. 768. New Haven, CT: Yale University.

Commander, S., A. Tolstopiatenko, and R. Yemtsov. (1997). "Channels of Redistribution: Inequality and Poverty in the Russian Transition." Paper presented at the European Bank for Reconstruction and Development "Inequality and Poverty in Transition Economies" Conference, May.

Davidson, R. and J. MacKinnon. (1981). "Several Tests for Model Specification in the Presence of Multiple Alternatives." *Econometrica* 49: 781–793.

De Melo, M., C. Denizer, and A. Gelb. (1996). "Patterns of Transition from Plan to Market." *World Bank Economic Review* 10 (3): 307–324.

Diamond, C. A., C. J. Simon, and J. T. Warner. (1990). "A Multinomial Probability Model of Size Income Distribution." *Journal of Econometrics* 43.

Einhorn, B. (1993). *Cinderella Goes to Market: Citizenship, Gender and Women's Movements in East Central Europe.* London: Verso.

Esping-Andersen, G. (1990). *The Three Worlds of Welfare Capitalism.* Princeton, NJ: Princeton University Press.

European Comparison Project. (1996). "Overall European Comparison Project 1993: Output Tables," mimeo.

Fabian, K. and J. D. Straussman. (1994). "Post-communist Transition of Local Government in Hungary: Managing Emergency Social Aid." *Public Administration and Development* 14: 271–280.

Fong, M. (1996). "Gender Barriers in the Transition to a Market Economy." Poverty and Social Policy Department Discussion Paper No. 87. Washington, DC: World Bank.

Foster, J., J. Greer, and E. Thorbecke. (1984). "A Class of Decomposable Poverty Measures." *Econometrica* 52: 571–576.

Funk, N. and M. Mueller. (1993). *Gender Politics and Post-Communism: Reflections from Eastern Europe and the Former Soviet Union.* New York: Routledge.

Gaiha, R. (1988). "On Measuring the Risk of Poverty in Rural India." Chapter 7 in T. N. Srinivasan and P. Bardhan (eds.), *Rural Poverty in South Asia.* New York: Columbia University Press.

Glewwe, P. (1991). "Investigating the Determinants of Household Welfare in the Côte d'Ivoire." *Journal of Development Economics* 35.

Glewwe P. and G. Hall. (1995). "Who Is Most Vulnerable to Macroeconomic Shocks? Hypotheses Tests Using Panel Data from Peru." Living Standards Measurement Study Working Paper No. 117. Washington DC: World Bank.

Goskomstat Rossii. (1995). *Statistical Yearbook of Russia 1995*. Moscow: Goskomstat Rossii.

Gregory, P. and R. Stuart. (1990). *Soviet Economic Structure and Performance*. New York: Harper & Row.

Grootaert, C. (1995). "Poverty and Social Transfers in Poland." Policy Research Working Paper No. 1440. Washington, DC: World Bank.

Grootaert, C. (1997a). "Poverty and Social Transfers in Hungary." Policy Research Working Paper No. 1770. Washington, DC: World Bank.

Grootaert, C. (1997b). "The Determinants of Poverty in Côte d'Ivoire in the 1980s." *Journal of African Economies* 6 (2): 169–196.

Grosh, M. and J. Baker. (1995). "Proxy Means Tests for Targeting Social Programs—Simulation and Speculation." Living Standards Measurement Study Working Paper No. 118. Washington, DC: World Bank.

Harris, J. and M. Todaro. (1970). "Migration, Unemployment, and Development: A Two-Sector Analysis." *American Economic Review* 60: 126–142.

Institute of Labor and Social Studies. (1994). "Social Policy and Social Conditions in Poland, 1989–1993." Occasional Papers No. 4.

Kaufmann, D. and A. Kaliberda. (1996). "Integrating the Unofficial Economy into the Dynamics of Post-Socialist Economies: A Framework of Analysis and Evidence." In B. Kaminski (ed.), *Economic Transition in Russia and the New States of Eurasia*. Armonk, NY: M.E. Sharpe.

Kingkade, W. (1993). "Demographic Prospects in the Republics of the Former Soviet Union." In U.S. Congress. Joint Economic Committee. *The Former Soviet Union in Transition* 2: 795–819. Washington, DC: US Government Printing Office.

Klugman, J. (1997). (Ed.) *Poverty in Russia: Public Policy and Private Responses*. Washington, DC: Economic Development Institute, World Bank.

Klugman J. and J. Braithwaite. (1998). "Poverty in Russia During the Transition: An Overview." *World Bank Research Observer* 13 (1).

Koen, V. (1996). "Russian Macroeconomic Data: Existence, Access, Interpretation." *Communist Economies and Economic Transformation* 8: 321–333.

Koen, V. and E. Gavrilenko. (1994). "How Large Was the Output Collapse in Russia? Alternative Estimates and Welfare Implications." International Monetary Fund Working Paper 94/6. Washington, DC: International Monetary Fund.

Kolev, A. (1996). "Poverty Analysis in Russia: What Can We Learn from the RLMS Round 6?" Florence, Italy: European University Institute.

Krumm, K., B. Milanovic and M. Walton. (1994). "Transfers and the Transition from Socialism: The Key Tradeoffs." Policy Research Working Paper No. 1380. Washington, DC: World Bank.

Lanjouw, P. and N. Stern. (1991). "Poverty in Palanpur." *World Bank Economic Review 5* (1).

Milanovic, B. (1990). "Poverty in Poland, Hungary, and Yugoslavia in the Years of Crisis 1978–87." Policy Research Working Paper No. 507. Washington, DC: World Bank.

Milanovic, B. (1995). "Poverty, Inequality and Social Policy in Transition Economies." *Transition Economies Research Paper No. 9.* Washington, DC: World Bank.

Milanovic, B. (1997). "Explaining the Growth in Inequality During the Transition." Mimeo. Policy Research Department. Washington, DC: World Bank.

Milanovic, B. (1998). *Income, Inequality, and Poverty During the Transition from Planned to Market Economy.* Regional and Sectoral Studies. Washington, DC: World Bank.

Perraudin, W. and T. Pujol. (1994). "Framework for the Analysis of Pension and Unemployment Benefits Reform in Poland." *International Monetary Fund Staff Papers* 41 (4): 643–674.

Ravallion, M. (1993). "Poverty Comparisons: A Guide to Concepts and Methods." *Living Standards Measurement Study Working Paper No. 88.* Washington, DC: World Bank.

Ravallion, M. (1996). "Issues in Measuring and Modeling Poverty." *The Economic Journal* 106: 1328–1343.

Revesz, T. (1994). "An Analysis of the Representativity of the Hungarian Household Budget Survey Samples." Mimeo. Department of Applied Economics. Cambridge, UK: Cambridge University.

Sipos, S. and I. G. Toth. (1998). "Social Transfers and Poverty Alleviation." In J.-J. Dethier and L. Bokros (eds.), *Public Finance Reform during the Transition: The Experience of Hungary.* Washington, DC: World Bank.

Subbarao, K., A. Bonnerjee, J. Braithwaite, S. Carvalho, K. Ezemenari, C. Graham, and A. Thompson. (1997). *Safety Net Programs and Poverty Reduction: Lessons from Cross-Country Experience.* Washington, DC: World Bank.

World Bank. (1993). *Poland: Income Support and the Social Safety Net During the Transition.* Washington, DC: World Bank.

World Bank. (1994a). *Averting the Old-Age Crisis.* Washington, DC: World Bank.

World Bank. (1994b). *Poland: Poverty in Poland.* Report No. 13051-POL. Washington, DC: World Bank.

World Bank. (1995a). *Kyrgyz Republic: Poverty Assessment and Strategy.* Report No. 14380-KG. Washington, DC: World Bank.

World Bank. (1995b). *Russia: Poverty in Russia: An Assessment.* Report No. 14110-RU. Washington, DC: World Bank.

World Bank. (1995c). *Ukraine: Poverty in Ukraine.* Report No. 15602-UA. Washington, DC: World Bank.

World Bank. (1995d). *Understanding Poverty in Poland.* Washington, DC: World Bank.

World Bank. (1996a). *Armenia: Confronting Poverty Issues.* Report No. 15693-AM. Washington, DC: World Bank.

World Bank. (1996b). *Belarus: An Assessment of Poverty and Prospects for Improved Living Standards.* Report No. 15380-BY. Washington, DC: World Bank.

World Bank. (1996c). *Estonia: Living Standards During the Transition.* Report No. 15637-EE. Washington, DC: World Bank.

World Bank. (1996d). *Hungary: Poverty and Social Transfers.* Report No. 14658-HU. Washington, DC: World Bank.

World Bank. (1996e). *World Development Report 1996: From Plan to Market.* Washington, DC: World Bank.

# Index

(italics indicate graph or table)